AN EQUAL START?

IMPROVING SUPPORT DURING PREGNANCY AND THE FIRST 12 MONTHS

Lisa Harker and Liz Kendall

ippr

30-32 Southampton Street, London WC2E 7RA
Tel: 020 7470 6100 Fax: 020 7470 6111
info@ippr.org
www.ippr.org
Registered charity 800065

The Institute for Public Policy Research (ippr), established in 1988, is Britain's leading independent think tank on the centre left. The values that drive our work include delivering social justice, deepening democracy, increasing environmental sustainability and enhancing human rights. Through our well-researched and clearly argued policy analysis, our publications, our media events, our strong networks in government, academia and the corporate and voluntary sector, we play a vital role in maintaining the momentum of progressive thought.

ippr's aim is to bridge the political divide between the social democratic and liberal traditions, the intellectual divide between the academics and the policy makers and the cultural divide between the policy-making establishment and the citizen. As an independent institute, we have the freedom to determine our research agenda. ippr has charitable status and is funded by a mixture of corporate, charitable, trade union and individual donations.

Research is ongoing, and new projects being developed, in a wide range of policy areas including sustainability, health and social care, social policy, citizenship and governance, education, economics, democracy and community, media and digital society and public private partnerships. In the future we aim to grow into a permanent centre for contemporary progressive thought, recognised both at home and globally.

For further information you can contact ippr's external affairs department on info@ippr.org, you can view our website at www.ippr.org and you can buy our books from Central Books on 0845 458 9910 or email ippr@centralbooks.com.

Trustees

Production & design by **EMPHASIS**
ISBN 1 86030 212 2
© IPPR 2003

Contents

Acknowledgements

The authors are very grateful to Wyeth, The Sutton Trust, The Nuffield Trust and Nutricia whose financial support enabled us to undertake this project.

During the course of writing this report Lisa Harker spent three months as a Visiting Research Fellow at the Department of Social Policy and Social Work, University of Oxford. Lisa is grateful to Teresa Smith and colleagues for their support during her sabbatical.

Equal at One is the final report of ippr's First 12 Months project and draws on the ideas outlined in a series of papers commissioned by ippr. These papers by Jane Naish, Anne Page and Fran Bennett are available on our website (www.ippr.org). We have benefited greatly from the thoughtful insights provided by the authors of these papers but we stress that the views expressed in this final report are entirely our own.

We are particularly grateful to Sarah Deacon and Deborah Katz who provided invaluable research assistance during the writing of this report. Many thanks are due to members of the project's advisory group who provided advice and support throughout the project: Adrienne Burgess, Jacky Chambers, Anna Coote, Naomi Eisenstadt, Louise Emanuel, Caroline Healy, Christine Gowdridge, Heather Joshi, Kathleen Kiernan, Ruth Lister, Margaret Lochrie, Jim McCormick, Anne Page, Djuna Thurley and Sheila Wolfendale.

We are grateful to others who have given us advice and comments: Val Buxton, Joe Hallgarten, Paul Harker, Mark Jones, Kathy Mumby-Croft, Rachel O'Brien, Carey Oppenheim, Megan Pacey, Gillian Pugh, Sue Regan and Matthew Taylor. We would also like to thank Helena Scott for her help in producing the report.

About the authors

Lisa Harker was Deputy Director at the Institute for Public Policy Research until April 2003 where she was responsible for overseeing IPPR's research programme and with the Director has oversight of the day-to-day management of the organisation. Her own research interests include tax and benefit policy, poverty, family policy and childcare. Until March 2000 Lisa was UK Advocacy Co-ordinator at Save the Children and previously worked for BBC News as Social Affairs Specialist and as Campaigns Team Co-ordinator at Child Poverty Action Group. She is Chair of Trustees at Daycare Trust and a former Executive Committee member of the Fabian Society.

Liz Kendall is an Associate Director at IPPR and responsible for running the Institute's programme of research on health and social care. She was previously the Fellow of the Public Health Programme at the King's Fund. From 1996 to 1998, Liz was a Special Adviser to the Rt Hon Harriet Harman, MP, Secretary of State for Social Security and Minister for Women.

We owe it to every child to unleash their potential. They are of equal worth. They deserve an equal chance...

There is no more powerful symbol of our politics than the experience of being on a maternity ward. Seeing two babies side by side. Delivered by the same doctors and midwives. Yet two totally different lives lie ahead of them.

One returns with his mother to a bed and breakfast that is cold, damp, cramped. A mother who has no job, no family to support her, sadder still: no one to share the joy and triumph of the new baby, a father nowhere to be seen. That mother loves her child like any other mother. But her life and her baby's life is a long, hard struggle. For this child, individual potential hangs by a thread.

The second child returns to a prosperous home, grandparents desperate to share the caring, and a father with a decent income and an even larger sense of pride. They're already thinking about schools, friends she can make, new toys they can buy. Expectations are sky high, opportunities truly limitless.

Tony Blair, speech to Labour Party Conference, 1999

The older principle of universality needs to be brought [back] alongside diversity. The starting point is our common humanity and the phenomena of birth, death, illness, work, happiness and loss. True, these are experienced differently, but the conditions are common: hence [TH] Marshall's proposition that 'when you are weighing a naked baby on the scales, the idea of social class does not obtrude itself greatly'.

P Harris, 'Welfare rewritten' *Journal of Social Policy* July 2002

Executive summary

Equal at one?

Few people would challenge the notion that society should aspire to an equal start for every child. But our commitment to equality at this stage of life is superficial unless we confront some of the difficult issues that arise. Three issues immediately present themselves. Firstly, even though they are of equal worth, children are not born equal. The economic circumstances, health, cognitive ability, personality traits and parental expectations of each newborn immediately place them on a hierarchy of life chances. A commitment to equality is therefore immediately challenged by the reality that parents provide very different circumstances for their children, materially, physically and genetically. Achieving an equal start is dependent upon a willingness to prevent (or compensate for) the disadvantage that begins well before birth.

Secondly, the natural instinct of parents to do the best for their children can also perpetuate inequality, given the unequal opportunities that are also open to parents. Persisting inequalities are in part a reflection of the unequal power of parents to act on the universal desire to achieve the best opportunities for their children.

And thirdly, a commitment to equality requires us to question the role of the State in influencing opportunities during the early months of life. The State's duty to protect children from neglect and child abuse is rarely questioned. Promoting the health of mother and child has long been a public policy objective, and in more recent times the State has played a significant role in helping to tackle poverty and deprivation. But less acknowledged, in public policy terms at least, is the profound impact that the parent-child relationship has on an infant's development.

If we are serious about giving children an equal start in life we cannot overlook the significance of parenting. Public policy must be more readily prepared to cross the threshold into the private world of the family, although this is a step that must be taken with great care. Too much interference in the relationship between a parent and child will be not only an infringement of individual liberty; it may, if handled inappropriately, be counter-productive.

Why pregnancy and the first twelve months matter

By the time a child reaches his or her first birthday, much of the foundation for the rest of life will be laid. The period from pregnancy through the first twelve months of life is a crucial stage of development. No other life stage is more risky, yet no other time offers greater opportunity for effective intervention.

The most hazardous period of life

As an affluent nation the UK enjoys a generally high standard of infant health and wellbeing. Nevertheless, the first year of life remains the most hazardous: mortality rates are highest around and just after birth. Over half the children who die as a result of child abuse each year do so as a baby.

Risk of ill health or mortality is not evenly spread throughout the population. Many children are born into pre-existing poverty, which can have a long-term impact on their development. Striking inequalities in infant mortality rates remain and in some cases have actually widened slightly in recent years. Social class remains one of the most significant predictors: a baby born into social class V is over twice as likely to die in the first year of life as one born into social class I.

The foundation of life

These inequalities matter because the early stages of life are critical in determining later development. It is the dynamic and complex relationship between nature (genes) and nurture (experience) that shapes human development. There is now a considerable body of evidence which suggests that early life experiences strongly influence the way the brain develops and that this can have a long-term impact on a child's development.

Parents' interactions with their children appear to have an important and lasting effect on this process. For example, the amount of verbal interaction parents have with their infants has been shown to influence language development and reading ability during later childhood, the effects of which may persist into adult life. Stark differences in cognitive ability emerge at a young age.

Parent-infant interactions are also crucial in shaping children's later social and emotional development. The quality of the parent/child interaction is particularly important because it enhances an infant's feelings of self-worth, self-esteem, a sense of belonging and a degree of control, which in turn can help protect them from the stress of social disadvantage.

What makes a difference?

The complexity of the world into which children are born defies a simple definition of the optimal environment for an infant to flourish. Nevertheless, research has identified consistent factors that appear to benefit or undermine healthy development. These factors are central to our search for greater equality in child outcomes and should determine the direction of public policy.

Prenatal factors

Among the most powerful predictors of child outcomes are those that are in evidence in parental circumstances before a child is born: parental education and employment, the financial circumstances of the family, and maternal and paternal health and wellbeing. The health of the mother-to-be is particularly important during pregnancy. An inadequate diet, smoking, alcohol and drug use, exposure to environmental hazards, depression and stress can all lead to poor developmental outcomes for children.

A child's cognitive development is also indirectly influenced by experience in utero. Low birth weight babies are more likely to grow up with a lower cognitive ability than babies born with a higher birth weight, even when socio-economic factors known to affect cognitive function are taken into account. Nevertheless the exact nature of the relationship between parental (particularly maternal) wellbeing during pregnancy and child health and cognitive functions remains uncertain.

Child abuse and neglect

Child abuse and neglect has an obvious direct and negative impact on child development. Although the risk of abuse is small, children under one are at the greatest risk of being placed on a child protection register and the homicide rate for under ones is almost five times greater than the average. The complexity of risk factors that are associated with child abuse and neglect suggest that all services that come into contact with parents and children should be attuned to the potential for children to be at risk. However, the most important steps in preventing child abuse and neglect will be to support parents in their parenting roles and with their relationship with one another.

Poverty

Growing up in a poor family has an immediate and long-term impact on a child's development. Children born into low income families are more likely to be of low birth weight (which is in itself a health risk), die in the first year of life and suffer significant episodes of illness such as respiratory infections. The long-term impact of poverty is also significant. Children growing up in poor households are more likely than their better-off peers to have low educational attainment, leave school at 16, have poor health, come into early contact with police, be unemployed as young adults, have low expectations for the future and end up earning a relatively low wage.

The relationship between poverty and detrimental outcomes is complex and many children who grow up in poverty do not experience health, behavioural, cognitive or emotional problems later in life. Children are more likely to be resilient in the face of adversity when they develop certain social and emotional skills. The role that a strong family environment can play in helping children to acquire these skills underlines the importance of supporting parenting as well as ameliorating the disadvantaging effects of poverty through tax and benefit policies.

Sweeping conclusions about the impact of maternal education and employment on children's development are misleading. Maternal education may be a important factor affecting early cognitive development because it can be a key determinant of the level of verbal interaction mothers have with their children. However there is no clear evidence as to whether improvements in maternal education after the birth of a child can have a direct impact on children's outcomes. The impact of maternal employment on child outcomes is even less clear (and the impact of paternal employment hardly ever explored).

Parenting style

A crucial feature of early child development is the acquisition of skills and experience that help infants face new or challenging situations, and provide an awareness of how to influence the world around them. The relationship between an infant and their caregiver is critical in this process. The key period during which an infant establishes stable relationships with those around them is between six to eighteen months.

The style of parenting that emerges during this period can have a long-term impact on a child's development. Children with more secure parental attachments appear less likely to be socially isolated and aggressive in pre-school and school.

Early parent-child interaction can also influence an infant's capacity for learning. During this early period the auditory centres of the brain are stimulated by the repeated sounds that infants hear and this can be important for later language development. Research suggests that the number and quality of early interactions between parents and their children can influence the development of critical neural pathways in the young brain.

Parental mental health is one of the factors most likely to influence a parent's interaction with an infant. Poor parental mental health is relatively common after the birth of a child and can affect the development of positive parenting skills. However, the link between parental depression and adverse child outcomes is by no means certain and successful treatment of depression can remove any adverse effects on a child's development.

While most research focuses on the mother-infant relationship, the father-infant relationship is often overlooked. Fathers now carry out one-third of parental childcare. Fathers' and mothers' involvement with children has been found to be of a different nature, particularly when their children are young. Despite this, it is thought that the gender of the parent is less important for child development than broader parenting style.

Childcare

A key concern has been whether entering childcare during the first year of life harms a child's ability to form secure attachments with adults.

The quality of childcare seems to be particularly important in relation to children from low-income families. This may be because the child care environment is more optimal (for example in terms of exposure to language) than the children's home environment.

The impact of public policy

Antenatal support

In the UK, women are offered a relatively high number of antenatal visits. There is some evidence to suggest that the number of antenatal visits could be reduced without risk to mother or baby.

The importance of the antenatal period in terms of personal support and preparation for parenthood, as opposed to traditional antenatal healthcare, has been comparatively overlooked, despite demonstrations of the potency of even short periods of such support. There have long been calls for better information and support for parents not simply about the process of giving birth but also about motherhood, fatherhood and the social and emotional changes they are likely to face.

Midwifery and health visiting

Of all the professionals that work with families during pregnancy and the first year of a child's life, midwives and health visitors are the most important. This is partly because of the level of contact they have with parents and children during the antenatal and postnatal period but it is also because of the adaptable and empowering ways in which these professionals can work.

However, the midwifery and health visiting workforce currently faces major capacity constraints. The highest ever vacancy rates were recorded in the 2002 Royal College of Midwives annual staffing survey, throwing into doubt the likelihood of the Government reaching its 2004 target of recruiting 2,000 more midwives. These problems are unlikely to abate in the near future since both midwifery and health visiting professions have an ageing workforce.

Despite the fact that midwives and health visitors both work with parents and children they rarely meet. They do not share a common identity and whilst they work with identical population groups, in practice they rarely exchange ideas and information about the population they work with and do not share a practice framework. The majority of midwives and health visitors have their caseloads organised by GP attachment, working to one or more GP practice, rather than on the basis of geographical area. This creates a tension with geographically defined services such as those provided under the auspices of Sure Start. Some have suggested bringing midwifery and health visiting closer together under the remit of Primary Care Trusts' public health teams.

Parenting programmes

There is now a variety of different parenting programmes available in the UK, including parenting education projects, counselling and therapy services, self-help groups and information services.

However, there services fall well short of providing universal support. One survey found that just under half of parents did not know where to go to get advice and help for family problems. Substantial gaps in provision have been identified, including support for minority ethnic families and (all) fathers, as well as support for families with disabled children, for teenage parents and for families with experience of mental health problems. Relationship support services are very poorly developed.

Evaluations of successful parenting programmes have shown that the best outcomes seem to be associated with programmes that start early, preferably during pregnancy, are continuous, occur with some intensity, take account of multiple factors, develop an appropriate alliance with parents, target the most needy, relate help to need, are home based and use well trained and supported staff. Centre-based educational interventions for children are associated with improved cognitive and language development and subsequent school achievement. Group based programmes have been shown to be both effective and cost-effective: community based parent training schemes may be up to six times as cost effective as individual clinic-based programmes.

Studies have reported that parents feel that there is insufficient information about what it is like to become a parent, too little advice about the 'pitfalls' that might be experienced and insufficient sources of immediate help and advice if they need reassurance and guidance.

Parents say that the support offered to them after the birth of a child can often be child-focused and insufficiently family-focused.

Parents seem to value the help, support, advice and feedback they get from non-experts, including their peers. Some studies have found no difference in outcomes between a well trained lay home visitor and an MSc level professional. Others question whether such workers are able to influence parenting behaviours arguing that their greatest strength instead lies in improving mothers' emotional wellbeing. Nevertheless, volunteer-based programmes such as Home-Start have been shown to be beneficial.

Childcare

For many children, the quality of the non-parental childcare they receive in the first year of life will be an important factor in their development. The introduction of the national childcare strategy in 1998 placed childcare higher on the political agenda than ever before. But change in childcare policy has come faster than change in practice. By 2001 there was one registered childcare place per seven children under eight years of age, compared to one per nine children in 1997. For younger children the level of childcare provision remains limited and expensive. Where good quality group-based care has been developed – such as in a number of Early Excellence Centres – it can provide an environment in which children can thrive.

Financial support and leave arrangements

In the past the UK has had comparatively low levels of financial support for parents. There has also been a significant financial penalty attached to motherhood, compared with many other industrialised countries.

However, a number of changes in financial support have been introduced in recent years. As part of attempts to meet a government commitment to eradicate child poverty in a generation, benefit levels have increased. By October 2002, income support rates for younger children had nearly doubled in real terms since 1997 and a new 'baby tax credit' was introduced in April 2002. Changes have also been made in relation to maternity leave. The UK now has the longest maternity leave in Europe but half of the leave entitlement is unpaid and the remainder is paid at a relatively low level of income replacement. The Sure Start Maternity Grant was introduced in 2000 to replace the maternity payment from the Social Fund. Unpaid time off for (emergency) family reasons, paternity leave and (unpaid) parental leave have also been introduced. But despite the case being made for years by maternity groups and others, there have been no moves to improve financial support for those on low incomes during pregnancy.

Reform of in-kind support for low-income families is currently under consultation in the UK. A new scheme is proposed – Healthy Start – which will include a broader range of foods such as fruit and vegetables, cereal-based food and other foods suitable for weaning. Moves towards working in partnership with parents might be undermined if professionals are given a greater role as gatekeepers for welfare benefits, as is being suggested under the Government's proposals to reform the Welfare Foods Scheme.

Improving support for parents and children

The combination of the Government's timidity in tackling inequality and a continued reticence about being seen to cross the threshold into the private world of the family is constraining progress on achieving more equal life chances for children. Both pose considerable challenges politically; but they are both crucial to achieving change.

Transforming health visiting and midwifery

The need for better workforce planning in the NHS and a strengthened recruitment drive for the health visiting and midwifery workforce is evident. However, more fundamental change may be needed if a younger generation of health visitors and midwives is to be attracted into the professions.

If midwives and health visitors are to be able to provide the social and emotional support to parents that research indicates is vital for child development, the nature of their role will need to change. They will need to move away from an approach based on child health monitoring and assessment to a more rounded role in supporting families; a move that is already taking place in some parts of the country as the profession enhances its public health role. This shift will require greater emphasis on the role that health visitors and midwives play in supporting adults in preparation for, and support during, parenthood.

Given the current shortage of health visitors and midwives, any broadening of their role at this time will be difficult to deliver. This brings into question the nature of the universal service that midwives and health visitors can realistically provide. There is a case for better targeting of resources to areas of high deprivation with the health visitor and midwifery workforce distributed according to measures of social deprivation indices as a proxy for need for health care – not simply on the basis of population size.

A new 'Home Visitor' service

In addition, the universal support that health visitors provide in the postnatal period will need to be supplemented with additional non-professional support in future.

One option would be to consider a new service to provide practical and emotional support for parents. A 'Home Visitor' service would consist of an 'on your side' advocate and mentor for parents, someone who would be able to provide regular and continuous support from the third trimester of pregnancy, during the early months of a child's life and potentially throughout the first year. A Home Visitor could be an experienced parent or grandparent or someone who has trained as a midwife or health visitor. They would take on a different role to health professionals in acting as a mentor and personal adviser – providing a gateway to a range of services for parents. Funding to encourage the development of Home Visitor support could be ring-fenced as part of the Government's plans for a £25 million parenting fund, as announced in the 2002 Spending Review.

Children's Centres

The Government has announced its intention to introduce children's centres in some of the most deprived areas in the country. Along with a range of services for children and parents, these centres would provide the focus for good quality childcare services in a locality. Children's centres could provide a one-stop centre for all parents, providing universal access to high quality provision for children of all ages, allowing for better co-ordination of all local services for children and engaging families and communities in their organisation and development.

Social security reform

Given the importance of pre-pregnancy health and diet, and the difficulty of targeting a prospective parent population, the adequacy of social security support for the under-25s should be reviewed. Preconception health status is crucial in determining the wellbeing of a child. Under-25 benefit rates for single childless people should be increased to the 25-plus level.

Evidence that financial support during pregnancy can lead to better child outcomes provides a compelling argument for the introduction of financial support in recognition of pregnancy. An additional premium should be paid to pregnant women receiving income support

Additional financial support should also be given to large families. The UK is unusual in providing relatively more generous support for one-child families. Yet the child poverty rate among six-child household is 71 per cent, by 2004 over half of children in low income families will be living in large families. Greater support for large families could be achieved by increasing the payments per child (for example in the child tax credit and/or child benefit for second or subsequent children) as a priority over increasing the rates per family.

The proposals to extend the Welfare Foods Scheme to a wider range of foods is welcome and in line with parents' own views. The change also rightly proposes equalisation of benefits between breastfeeding and non-breastfeeding mothers, although without increasing the financial value of the support there is scepticism as to whether the scheme will make a significant difference to the nutrition of poor mothers and children. The link between health advice and registration for the scheme is more contentious. While the desired outcome (better health of children and parents) is laudable, using the benefits system to try and achieve this aim is problematic because it may undermine parents' sense of control over their own circumstances and have a negative impact on the professional-client relationship.

Improving leave arrangements

Further improvements to maternity pay are needed if the risk of poverty associated with having a child is to be reduced and mothers are to have genuine choices about whether to return to work or not in the first year of their child's life.

The UK Government must take action to encourage a more equal sharing of parental responsibilities in the first year of life. Various steps are needed. Paternity leave should be lengthened; but the priority must be to pay it at a higher level. Earnings-related payment (up to a ceiling) for parental leave should be introduced. The limit on the number of weeks of parental leave (up to a maximum level) that can be taken in the first year should be abolished. For two-parent families, once parental leave is paid, some period should be reserved for fathers. This 'daddy quota' could be given on a 'use it or lose it' basis, so that it is forgone if fathers do not take it.

Conclusion

All those who wish to achieve a more socially just society must concern themselves with reducing the unequal life chances that emerge soon after birth but this raises difficult issues for progressive politics, such as the power of inherited privilege and the tension between parents' liberty to do the best for their children and the desire to achieve a fairer share of opportunities.

Policy makers also face a more immediate challenge; that of paying greater attention to factors that shape a child's development during and after birth. The profound impact that the parent-child relationship has on an infant's development has tended to be overlooked in public policy. Yet if we want to encourage the optimal circumstances in which children can achieve an equal start in life, policy makers must consider ways in which social and emotional support for parents can be improved.

While an individual's development is by no means set for life, their capacity to benefit from life opportunities is significantly enhanced by positive experiences in the early months of life. Without a step change in the quantity and quality of support for parents and children during this crucial period of development, an equal start for children will remain no more than a worthy statement of ambition.

1. An equal start: an ambitious agenda

It is difficult to imagine a more potent measure of a progressive society than the achievement of an equal start for every child. It is the foundation of a good society. It reflects not only the belief that individuals are inherently of equal worth but it is also a prerequisite for the pursuit of equality of opportunity. For equality of opportunity to have any meaning it must rest on the presumption that all individuals begin life with the same chances.

An equal start for children is an aspiration that at first sight appears uncontested. We are more committed to equality at birth than at any other time in the lifecycle. We consider all newborns to be of equal status; our prejudices about one another tend to emerge later. Moreover, unlike most debates about equality, there is no expectation that newborns should be rewarded for their own particular effort or abilities. The need to disentangle those inequalities that arise from differences in talents, skills and hard work from those that arise from unfair circumstances is avoided.

But our commitment to an equal start for children is at best superficial. It lacks clarity about what equality in the early months of life really means and it is diluted by an unwillingness to face the challenge of how it might be achieved.

The gap between a notional commitment to equality at birth and its realisation is partly due to a misplaced fear that equality is about achieving blanket uniformity. An equal start in life is not about achieving the same experiences for all children or making all children alike. Our concern must be to address the unjust inequalities – inequalities in health, cognitive ability and emotional wellbeing – that emerge early in life and cannot be justified on the grounds of individual talents or efforts alone. Reductions in such inequalities are the measures by which we should judge the wellbeing of our society: they are the 'outcomes' that partially reflect the success (or failure) to build the foundations of a good society.

Our ambition for an equal start requires us to face up to difficult truths. Firstly, even though they are of equal worth, children are not born equal. To a great extent the trajectory of our lives is set before we are born. A child's inheritance – the economic circumstances, health, cognitive ability, personality traits and parental expectations of each newborn – immediately place them on a hierarchy of life chances. A commitment to equality is therefore immediately challenged by the reality that parents provide (materially, physically and genetically) very different circumstances for their children. The power of inherited privilege remains the biggest obstacle to equality. Achieving an equal start is dependent upon a willingness to prevent (or compensate for) the disadvantage that begins well before birth.

The almost universal desire to achieve the best outcomes for children can be an obstacle to, as well as a catalyst for, achieving greater equality. At one level the fact that all parents want the best for their children can offer hope for the fulfilment of an equal start for every child. But the natural instinct of parents to do the best for their children can also perpetuate inequality, given the unequal opportunities that are also open to parents. Advances in new health technologies may exacerbate inequalities in future. Pre-implementation genetic diagnosis may present the opportunity to avoid future generations having 'undesirable' characteristics. Technologies may also allow the modification of significant parts of our genetic make-up. For parents who wish to achieve the best for their children (and have the means to afford it) such technologies may prove irresistible. While such issues lie beyond the scope of this book, it is nevertheless important to acknowledge that persisting inequalities are in part a reflection of the unequal power of parents to act on the universal desire to achieve the best opportunities for their children, and that future technological developments are likely to exacerbate this trend.

A commitment to an equal start for children also requires us to question the role of the State in influencing opportunities during the early months of life. The State's duty to protect children from neglect and child abuse is rarely questioned. Promoting the health of mother and child has long been a public policy objective, and in more recent times the State has played a significant role in helping to tackle poverty and deprivation. But less acknowledged, in public policy terms at least, is the profound impact that the parent-child relationship has on an infant's development. This is an area in which the State has chosen to tread carefully, reluctant to interfere in the private realm of family life other than in the most desperate of circumstances.

Yet from the earliest months of life, the pattern of interaction between a parent and child – heavily influenced by a parent's own wellbeing – has a lasting impact on an infant's social and emotional development. The relationship between parents and their babies is particularly important in shaping social and emotional development but can also help protect young children from the stress of social disadvantage. It is clear that we have underestimated the impact of the social milieu of the family during early childhood in the past (Esping Anderson 2003).

If we are serious about giving children an equal start in life we cannot overlook the significance of parenting. Public policy must be more readily prepared to cross the threshold into the private world of the family, although this is a step that must be taken with great care. Too much interference in the relationship between a parent and child will be not only an infringement of individual liberty; it may, if handled inappropriately, be counter-productive. Public policy will fail if it is perceived as an uninvited intervention – an imposition on the otherwise private life of parenting.

This book considers how public policy should change in order to achieve a more equal start for children. Research in this field has tended to focus on isolated areas of public policy support. Yet there is a need to improve our understanding of the complex interconnected factors that influence life circumstances (Hobcraft 2002). So here we consider a wide range of policy interventions, including financial, health and parenting support, and assess the appropriate balance between them. We have set aside some questions for future work, such as how the impact of inherited wealth might be reduced. Our focus here is specifically on how public policy interventions during pregnancy and the first year of life need to be re-balanced to tackle inequalities during the early years.

In rightly seeking to achieve greater equality for children we must, however, avoid being over prescriptive about children's lives. It is important to recognise the dangers of perceiving children as empty vessels into which the right ingredients must be poured to create optimal adults. As Marina Warner warned in her 1994 Reith Lecture 'the depth of adult investment in a utopian childhood state...can [only] lead to disillusion'. An overly prescriptive approach to early childhood is dangerous not only because it has eugenic overtones, but because it is unlikely to be successful in achieving better outcomes since the impact of different factors on child development is highly complex and yet to be fully understood.

In failing to achieve greater equality in the first 12 months of life, we undermine our ability to achieve greater equality at any other point in our lives: such is the powerful influence of the early years on our life chances. A vision of greater equality in the first year of life is therefore not only about achieving better outcomes for children, it is vital to the pursuit of the good society.

2. Why pregnancy and the first 12 months matter

By the time a child reaches his or her first birthday, much of the foundation for the rest of life will be laid. Pregnancy and the first twelve months is a crucial period of development. It is a time of hazard and hope. No other life stage is more risky, yet no other time offers greater opportunity for effective intervention. In terms of achieving greater equality, no period of life matters more than pregnancy and the first 12 months.

The most hazardous period of life

As an affluent nation the UK enjoys a generally high standard of infant health and wellbeing. Improvements in living standards and medical advances mean that infant mortality rates have declined to 5.6 per thousand births (in England and Wales). Nevertheless, the first year of life remains the most hazardous: mortality rates are highest around and just after birth and nearly 3,500 infants die (in England and Wales) each year before they are one year old.

Congenital abnormalities are often a cause of death around the time of birth but the home environment and material circumstances are also significant. Some of the risk factors associated with this period lie very much in parents' hands: over half of all children who die as a result of child abuse each year do so as a baby. However, circumstances that lie beyond parents' control alone are also significant. Many children are born into pre-existing poverty; their parents are already living on a very low income when they are born. Over 200,000 families – nearly one in three of those having babies each year – are eligible for a Sure Start maternity grant because they are living on a low income. The birth of a child also increases the risk of poverty. A significant minority (one in three) of households experience a fall in living standards on the birth of a baby, and up to one in six (between 10 and 15 per cent) fall into poverty as a result (HM Treasury 1999). Families are not only more likely to be in poverty when their children are young but very young children are at particular risk of being poor for long periods (Hill and Jenkins 1999).

Growing up in poverty has a long-term impact on child development and later adult opportunities. Sixty years ago the publication of Richard Titmuss' report *Birth Poverty and Wealth* was greeted with the newspaper headline 'poor folks babies stand less chance' (cited in Roberts 1997). In spite of the significant social and medical progress that has been made in the past sixty years, today's evidence prompts a similar conclusion.

As shown in Figure 2.1, infant mortality rates are higher among those population groups more likely to be living on a low income. Social class remains one of the biggest predicting factors. A baby born into social class V is over twice as likely to die in the first year of life as one born into social class I (ONS 2000). Despite improvements to health and living standards striking inequalities in infant mortality rates according to social class have not only remained but have recently widened slightly (Health Statistics Quarterly Winter 2001).

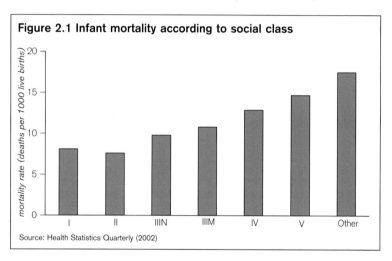

Figure 2.1 Infant mortality according to social class

mortality rate (deaths per 1000 live births)

Source: Health Statistics Quarterly (2002)

The infant mortality rate is higher in babies of mothers who are likely to be living alone (those registering the birth alone) than in the population as a whole. Infant mortality rates are also higher among babies born to mothers from the Indian subcontinent living in the UK (Balarajan and Releigh 1993), attributed in part to low birth weight associated with poor nutrition. Babies of mothers born in Pakistan have an infant mortality rate double that of the average in the UK population (*Health Statistics Quarterly* 2001).

These social class and racial inequalities are also reflected in regional differences in England. Infant mortality rates are 40-50 per cent higher in the North, North West, Yorkshire and the West Midlands than the

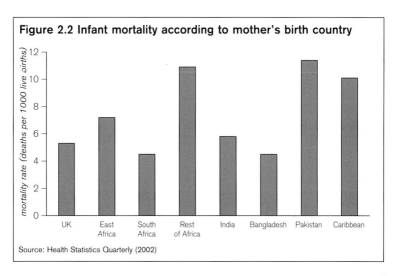

Figure 2.2 Infant mortality according to mother's birth country

Source: Health Statistics Quarterly (2002)

South East (excluding London) and South West. The differences look even more dramatic when considered at the level of the health authority. A baby born in Bradford is 10 times more likely to die in infancy compared to a baby born in Herefordshire (ONS 2000).

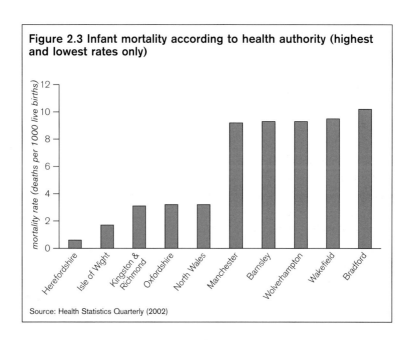

Figure 2.3 Infant mortality according to health authority (highest and lowest rates only)

Source: Health Statistics Quarterly (2002)

Similar social class differences can be detected for the majority of congenital abnormalities, with children of parents from manual social classes facing an increased risk of congenital anomalies such as cerebral palsy, asthma and heart disease (Drever and Whitehead 1997). There is also extensive evidence of social class differences in respiratory illness (Saxena *et al* 1999) and infectious disease (Reading 1997).

Low birth weight is associated with a higher risk of infant mortality and greater likelihood of health problems in childhood and adulthood (Acheson 1998) as well as lower cognitive ability, even when socio-economic factors known to affect cognitive function are taken into account (Richards *et al* 2001). Inequalities in birth weight therefore lie behind many of the other inequalities that emerge early in life, which in turn can have a lasting effect.

One in 12 babies born into social class V are low birth weight compared to one in 16 babies born into social class I (ONS 1997). Babies with families of social classes IV and V have a birth weight that is on average 130 grams lower than babies with families in social classes I and II. There is also a higher risk of low birth weight among certain ethnic minorities. Both first and second generation babies born in the UK to mothers from the Indian subcontinent face a high risk of low birth weight (Margetts *et al* 2002). This suggests that the environmental benefits of living in the UK have not been sufficient to reduce the risk of low birth weight among this group.

The foundation for life

The early stages of life are critical in determining later development. Genetic endowment is part of the equation. New discoveries emerging from the human genome project are increasing our understanding of the extent of our genetic inheritance. However, they are also revealing that our make-up is not hard-wired in our genetic code. Rather, it is the dynamic and complex relationship between nature (genes) and nurture (experience) that shapes human development.

Pregnancy and the first 12 months are a profoundly significant period in determining this relationship. One important example is the way the brain develops. Whilst some have contested the evidence that the early months are a 'critical period' for brain development (Wilson 2002) there is now a considerable body of evidence which suggests that early life experiences strongly influence the way the brain develops and that this can have a long-term impact.

Parents' interactions with their children appear to have an important and lasting effect on this process. For example, the amount of verbal interaction parents have with their infants has been shown to influence language development and reading ability during later childhood (Hart and Risley 1995) the effects of which may persist into adult life. Stark differences in cognitive ability emerge at a young age. Research has found a 14 percentage point difference in cognitive development between children from social classes 1 and 2 compared with those from social classes IV and V by the age of 22 months (Feinstein 1998). Although the wiring of the brain is not a once-only process and we continue to learn and relearn during life, the early years of life clearly have a profound effect.

Parent-infant interactions are also crucial in shaping children's later social and emotional development. It is during the earliest period of life that the pattern of parenting is established and the nature of the parent-infant relationship is formed. The quality of the parent/child interaction is particularly important because it enhances an infant's feelings of self-worth, self-esteem, a sense of belonging and a degree of control, which in turn can help protect them from the stress of social disadvantage. In the rare situations in which infants do not have the opportunity to form an attachment with a trusted adult, their development can deteriorate rapidly and dramatically (James 2002).

A wide range of other developments during pregnancy and the first twelve months can help lay the foundations for later life. During this period, children may be exposed to risk factors, such as poverty, abuse and neglect, but also to protective factors which can aid healthy development. Vital vaccination programmes, which prevent the onset of diseases like diptheria, whooping cough, polio and meningitis C, take place before children reach the age of one. Parents' actions, again, play a crucial role during this period. For example, research demonstrates that breastfeeding not only decreases the risk of infant mortality and the incidence and severity of infections during infancy and later childhood, but may also protect children against a range of illnesses during adult life (Acheson 1998). Recent research suggests that cognitive development may also be linked to breast-feeding (Angelsen *et al* 2001).

Early intervention is important

It must be emphasised that the links between early childhood and later outcomes are in no sense deterministic. The idea that it might be possible to accurately identify all children 'at risk' of adverse outcomes and intervene to prevent problems from ever coming into being is beguiling but ultimately flawed. Risk is certainly not destiny.

Nevertheless pregnancy and the first year of life offer the most important opportunity to intervene to reduce the risks that undermine healthy child development and to increase the potential for children to thrive. While an individual's development is by no means set for life – and later experiences can either undermine or ameliorate early development – an individual's capacity to overcome adversity and benefit from life opportunities is significantly enhanced by positive experiences in the early months of life.

The evidence that early childhood is influential in terms of subsequent healthy development (both physical and mental), educational attainment, employability, income potential or behavioural characteristics (Kuh and Ben-Shlomo 1997; Schweinhart *et al* 1993; Bradshaw 2001a) suggests that early intervention is likely to have the biggest impact on life chances. Unsurprisingly, those who are concerned about how to improve the health, educational and social wellbeing of society are most likely to note that the earlier the intervention the more effective (and cost-effective) it is.

3. What makes a difference?

The complexity of the world into which children are born defies a simple definition of the optimal environment for an infant to flourish. Even if we try to account for genetic inheritance and the influence of the physical, social and psychological circumstances into which children are born, the individual differences between them can astound us. Some children appear to thrive against all the odds.

Nevertheless, research has identified consistent factors that appear to benefit or undermine healthy development. These factors are central to our search for greater equality in child outcomes and should determine the direction of public policy.

Among the most important risk factors to an infant's early development are maternal ill health during pregnancy, abuse and neglect, poverty and deprivation and a difficult or damaged relationship between a parent and infant. An infant's early experience is largely based in the home but since two-thirds of women who are in a job when they become pregnant return to paid employment within ten months of the birth (DTI 2000), other factors such as the quality of childcare can be influential. In this chapter we look at each of these issues in turn to explore the extent and nature of their impact on a child's development.

Preconception, pregnancy and the postnatal period

Among the most powerful predictors of child outcomes are those that are in evidence in parental circumstances before a child is born: parental education and employment, the financial circumstances of the family, and maternal and paternal health and wellbeing.

Unsurprisingly, the health of the mother-to-be is particularly important during pregnancy. Two principal determinants of a baby's weight at birth (and subsequent health) are the mother's pre-pregnant weight and her own birth weight. For example, children of women who are underweight are at increased risk of developing non-insulin diabetes and raised blood pressure in adult life (Ravelli *et al* 1998; Clarke *et al* 1998).

A healthy pregnancy is likely to lead to better outcomes for children. An inadequate diet, smoking, alcohol and drug use, exposure to environmental hazards, depression and stress can all lead to poor developmental outcomes for children. Smoking during pregnancy, for example, is associated with reduced birth weight and increased risk of cot death (Blair *et al* 1996).

A child's cognitive development is also indirectly influenced by experience in utero. Low birth weight babies are more likely to grow up with a lower cognitive ability than babies born with a higher birth weight, even when socio-economic factors known to affect cognitive function are taken into account (Jefferis *et al* 2002).

But the exact nature of the relationship between parental (particularly maternal) wellbeing during pregnancy and child health and cognitive functions remains uncertain. In particular the relative importance of pre-conception and in utero experience to post conception experience is not yet fully understood.

Key to understanding the relative importance of preconception and prenatal intervention is new research that considers the risks to, and later consequences of, brain development during gestation. Risk factors believed to be associated with in utero brain development include maternal smoking, drug or alcohol use, exposure to toxic agents such as radiation, obstetric complications such as sustained oxygen reduction, and psychosocial stress. Some scientists believe that a number of neurological conditions (ranging from subtle deficiencies in learning ability to schizophrenia) may also be linked to in utero risk factors.

However, the evidence on these links is often contradictory, and therefore highly contested. Despite the vast literature exploring the relationship between in utero risk factors, brain development and later nervous system disorders, the research raises more questions than it answers. The relative significance of prenatal complications to later illness and the extent to which environmental factors in the womb interact with genetic risk for disease are particularly unclear.

During the immediate postnatal period, breastfeeding is highly beneficial for infant health, decreasing the incidence and severity of infections. Human milk contains a range of nutrients that seem to play a crucial role in protecting children against adverse outcomes in later life. Premature babies fed with breast milk are less likely to suffer from high blood pressure in adulthood and it is possible that all babies could benefit in a similar way (Singhal *et al* 2001). Breastfeeding also seems to aid cognitive development. Children who are breastfed for less than six months have been found to achieve lower cognitive scores between the aged of one and five than children who are breastfeed for six months or more (Angelsen *et al* 2001).

Not every mother is able, or chooses, to breastfeed and feeding infants with supplemented infant formula can lead to better outcomes for children compared to unmodified cows milk. For example, ij14

ron deficiency in infants is associated with developmental delay and providing iron supplemented infant formula in place of unmodified cows milk can help prevent iron deficiency (Booth and Aukett 1997).

In making decisions about priorities for public policy it is important to acknowledge the limits to our understanding of the complex range of factors that are likely to have an impact on child development, particularly during the preconception and prenatal periods. However, there is no doubt that improving the health of the population, particularly the health of pregnant women and women of childbearing age, will be crucial to the successful development of future generations of children (Acheson 1998).

Abuse and neglect

That child abuse and neglect have a detrimental impact on a child's development is obvious. Proportionately, the risk of abuse is small: around 3,000 infants under one are placed on the child protection register in England and Wales each year. However, children under the age of one are at the greatest risk of being placed on the register (Department of Health 2001) and the homicide rate for under ones is almost five times greater than the average (Home Office 2003). For these reasons there is a special need to consider how best to prevent child neglect and abuse during the first year of life.

The most likely perpetrators of child abuse and neglect are parents, although the associated risk factors are complex. Parental mental ill health and a range of social and economic factors (often associated with emotional stress and depression) are associated with an increased risk of child abuse. However, since only a small proportion of the parents who exhibit risk factors will actually abuse (or even kill) a baby, targeting interventions at the most vulnerable is extremely difficult.

The risk of damage resulting from physical punishment of an infant under the age of one is surprisingly high. Subdural haematoma, often resulting from an infant being shaken, is found in around one in 4,000 children under one (NSPCC 2002) and is associated with a mortality rate as high as 25 per cent and a morbidity rate of 50 per cent. Between 50 and 75 per cent of parents smack their children at this age (Smith 1995; Nobes and Smith 1997). The fragility of infants and the ease with which parents can damage a child is often poorly understood, although there have been moves to raise awareness through educational campaigns.

The complexity of risk factors that are associated with child abuse and neglect suggest that all services that come into contact with parents and children should be attuned to the potential for children to be at risk. Improvements could be made to the co-ordination of responses across a range of professions (Kendall and Harker 2002). However, the most important steps in preventing child abuse and neglect will be to support parents in their parenting roles, their relationships with babies and with one another.

Poverty and deprivation

Growing up in a poor family has an immediate and long-term impact on a child's development. Children born into low income families are more likely to be of low birth weight (which is in itself a health risk), die in the first year of life or suffer significant episodes of illness such as respiratory infections (Spencer 2000). The long-term impact of poverty is also significant. Children growing up in poor households are more likely than their better-off peers to have low educational attainment, leave school at 16, have poor health, come into early contact with police, be unemployed as young adults, have low expectations for the future and end up earning a relatively low wage (Gregg, Harkness and Machin 1999; McCulloch and Joshi 1999; Bradshaw 2001a; Ermisch *et al* 2001).

Living in poverty can mean an infant being denied basic needs such as warmth and nutrition. In addition poverty restricts a family's ability to participate in everyday activities, limiting aspirations as well as educational and recreational activities. In addition, poverty can also have a deleterious impact on parents' opportunities and their emotional wellbeing and these in turn can have an impact on a child's development.

It has been argued that poverty during the early years of a child's life is particularly harmful as it is more powerfully predictive of later achievement than poverty at any subsequent stage of development (Shonkoff and Phillips 2000). While we know that the first year of life is very important in terms of a child's development, few studies have isolated the direct impact of income poverty during these first few months. However, studies involving older children have identified a direct link between poverty and child outcomes. Evidence from two Canadian surveys (the National Longitudinal Survey of Children and Youth and the National Population Health Survey) have shown a clear link between family income and 27 different factors that are critical to child wellbeing, including learning capacity, behaviour and health status. For 80 per cent of these factors, child outcomes improved substantially as annual family income rose (Ross and Roberts 1999).

In the UK evidence from the 1970 British Cohort Study suggests that at least a third of the raw correlation between family income and educational attainment is due to the effect of income alone (Blanden *et al* 2001). Both Canadian and UK findings appear to be supported by the experience of US welfare programmes. This suggests that encouraging mothers to take up employment without additional in-work financial support rarely has a significant effect on child outcomes (Duncan and Chase-Landsdale 2000).

While such evidence suggests that poverty can have a direct impact on a child's development, the impact of poverty on parents, and therefore indirectly on children, is likely to be as crucial. For example, lack of income can limit a mother's diet during pregnancy, which (as we have already seen has a significant impact on a child's development. Increasing a mother's level of income during pregnancy has been shown to help reduce the likelihood of low birth weight. In a study undertaken between 1970 and 1974 in Gary, Indiana in the United States, low-income mothers who received a guaranteed minimum income during pregnancy were found to have heavier babies than those who did not receive additional financial support (Keher and Wolin 1979).

The impact of poverty and disadvantage on parents' mental health is also significant. (The issue of parental mental health is returned to below.) Parental depression is strongly linked to children's behavioural problems and low cognitive ability. Mothers in disadvantaged families are more likely to suffer from depression but less likely to have their condition detected. Evidence from Canada suggests that children in low income families are over three times as likely to be living with a parent who exhibits frequent signs of depression as children in high income families (Ross and Roberts 1999).

The relationship between poverty and detrimental outcomes is complex. The links between the experiences of child poverty and medium and long-term child outcomes, and the intervening effects of the family, local services and neighbourhoods, are not well understood (Plewis *et al* 2001). However, all the available evidence points to the same conclusion: increasing the level of a family income can help improve children's life chances.

This report has already stressed that the associations between poverty, disadvantage and later outcomes are in no sense deterministic. Many children who grow up in poverty do not experience health, behavioural, cognitive or emotional problems later in life. Low socio-economic status reduces the chances of success rather than leading inevitably to diminished attainment.

Factors such as the presence of dependable caregivers, self-confidence and self-esteem, a sense of optimism and control, the capacity to reflect and solve problems and clear aspirations have all been found to be important in determining a child's resilience. One longitudinal study in Australia found that a third of children who experienced chronic adversity from a young age went on to succeed at school, find meaningful employment and establish positive relationships with their immediate family, peers, teachers and neighbours. The children who were resilient in the face of disadvantage were found to have strong attachments to their primary caregiver (not necessarily a parent), an 'easy' temperament and above average intelligence. They also received a considerable amount of positive attention and had three or fewer siblings, with children spaced by at least two years (Werner 1997).

So the evidence suggests that children are more likely to be resilient in the face of adversity when they develop certain social and emotional skills. The role that a strong family environment can play in helping children to acquire these skills underlines the importance of supporting parenting as well as seeking to ameliorate the disadvantaging effects of poverty through tax and benefit policies.

Maternal education and employment

Maternal education may be a particularly important factor affecting early cognitive development because it can be a key determinant of the level of verbal interaction mothers have with their children. Children's test scores have been found to be strongly related to a mother's level of education, even after controlling for income (McCulloch and Joshi 1999). However there is no clear evidence as to whether improvements in maternal education after the birth of a child can have a direct impact on children's outcomes. One US study found that improving maternal education had no impact on young children's achievement scores, but another found that an additional year of maternal schooling during the child's first three years had a significant positive effect on children's vocabulary (Rosenzwig and Wolpin 1994).

The impact of maternal employment on child outcomes is even less clear (and the impact of paternal employment hardly ever explored). In the US, researchers have tended to find an adverse association between employment begun in the first year of a child's life and a child's development, both in terms cognitive development and behavioural adjustment, but there is also evidence to the contrary.

In the UK, Joshi and Verropoulou (2000) examined the impact of maternal employment during a child's first year on maths and reading and emotional adjustment scores at school age and later, using data from the National Child Development (second generation) Study. They found that poorer outcomes were associated with early maternal employment but that this was only statistically significant for reading scores. Small positive associations with later outcomes were found when mothers re-entered employment after their child was one year old. While there was some evidence for a detrimental impact of a mother working before her child is one year old, the study concluded that poor economic circumstances in the home and the mother's own academic ability and attainments were more important predictors of child academic and aggression scores.

Other research suggests the circumstances of the work mothers undertake and its impact on maternal wellbeing matter more than mothers' employment per se. Non-standard working hours, especially long hours during the first year of life, may pose a risk for child development, especially when combined with poor quality childcare.

How mothers feel about working during the first year of their child's life also appears to be critical to children's outcomes. In the US, Hoffman *et al* (1999) found that the positive effects of work on a mother's sense of wellbeing may be crucial in providing later advantages for children. In this country, Kiernan (1996) has shown a positive association between lone mothers' employment when children are teenagers and children's qualifications, suggesting this may be due to the effect of positive role models.

Sweeping conclusions about the impact of maternal education and employment on children's development are misleading. It appears that there may be an association between a mother's level of education attainment and a child's cognitive development. But improving educational attainment in the wider population may be as (if not more) effective as education programmes targeted at new mothers. The impact of maternal employment appears to be especially complex. Maternal employment during a child's first year may be associated with a slightly higher risk of poor child development outcomes but the evidence is not sufficiently compelling to suggest that maternal employment should be discouraged during this period of a child's life. Indeed, any negative impact needs to be balanced by the positive impact that maternal employment has on family income and parental self-esteem. In contrast to the well-trodden analysis of the affect of maternal employment, the impact of paternal employment on child development remains largely a mystery.

Parent-child interaction

A crucial feature of early child development is the acquisition of skills and experience that help infants face new or challenging situations, and provide an awareness of how to influence the world around them. The relationship between an infant and their caregiver is critical in this process. The key period during which an infant establishes stable relationships with those around them is between six to eighteen months. Well before their first birthday, infants exhibit clear preferences for, and special responsiveness to, certain adults (Shonkoff and Phillips 2000).

The style of parenting that emerges during this period can have a long-term impact on a child's development. Healthy child development is associated with what has become known as 'positive parenting'.

Positive parenting styles are seen as being warm and affectionate, predictable and consistent, recognising and emphasising good qualities, and being responsive to children's needs whilst at the same time setting clear limits. Concomitantly, 'negative' parenting styles are usually seen as providing harsh and inconsistent discipline, being highly critical and rejecting, neglectful and lacking in supervision.

The impact of the parent-child relationship on emotional and behavioural development may only become apparent later in childhood. Some research suggests that behaviour problems of clinical severity are evident in as many as one in five children (Patterson *et al* 2002). Children with more secure parental attachments appear less likely to be socially isolated and aggressive in pre-school and school. Conversely, various forms of insecure attachment, resulting from a lack of emotional engagement between parent and infant, can have long-term consequences, for example in increasing the likelihood of a child developing attention deficit hyperactivity disorder (ADHD) and other disruptive behaviours.

Early parent-child interaction can also influence an infant's capacity for learning. The amount of verbal interaction that infants have with their parents influences language development and later reading ability. During this period the auditory centres of the brain are stimulated by the repeated sounds that infants hear and this can be important for later language development (Logue 2001). As this report has already outlined, social class differences in language ability in young children have been traced to the quantity and variety of language to which children are exposed (Hart and Risley 1995).

We are only beginning to understand the mechanisms that link parent-child interactions and developmental outcomes. There is some emerging evidence that early interactions have a direct impact on brain development. Research suggests that the number and quality of early interactions between parents and their children influence the development of critical neural pathways in the young brain (Thatcher *et al* 1997). Connections are built from experience. Experiences that are repeated often appear to have a significant impact on how the brain is 'wired', with repeated, daily actions and interactions having the most effect.

During the early years of life, a child's brain is customised to match his or her daily experiences and the nature of these sensory experiences can affect how the brain develops, which in turn affects subsequent behaviour and learning (Chugani 1997). For example, it has been suggested that troubled early relationships can cause a child's brain to consume glucose to deal with stress, when glucose would otherwise be used for cognitive activity (Evans 2002). Early and repeated exposure to stress or violence can cause the brain to reorganise so as to increase receptor sites for alertness to chemicals, which in turn may be linked to later impulsiveness and aggression (Logue 2001).

The influence of the relationship between parent and child during the early months of life has often been overlooked in public policy. Yet the evidence suggests that the style of parenting behaviour established during this period may have a profound impact on later child development and that the effects may persist into adult life. It also appears that a positive family environment may be crucial for children to demonstrate resilience in the face of adversity. For these reasons, we should be paying greater attention to the ways in which parenting support during the early months of life could be improved.

Parental mental health

Parental mental health is one of the factors most likely to influence a parent's interaction with an infant. Poor parental mental health is relatively common after the birth of a child. The arrival of a new baby is a stressful event that can have a deleterious impact on emotional wellbeing and on a couple's relationship. Indeed, research suggests that the birth of a child can be a common trigger for relationship problems (McAllister 1995) and the way parents manage their relationship as a couple can have an impact on child development (Cowan and Cown 2000). In some cases emotional wellbeing can deteriorate significantly. Postnatal depression occurs among 10 to 15 per cent of mothers during the first year following birth – a time of intense mother-child interaction. Its peak onset is typically between two and four weeks after delivery, often lasting for six months and sometimes up to a year if left untreated.

The precise interaction between different forms of parental depression (including postnatal depression), early attachment and child development is yet to be fully understood. Nevertheless there is evidence of poor parenting skills among depressed mothers, including less attentive behaviour. One consequence of inattentive parenting may be that babies learn that their responses 'don't matter'. Such parenting has been consistently associated with poorer child outcomes (James 2002) and there is some evidence that poor parental mental health can influence early brain activity in infants and long-term behavioural outcomes (Dawson *et al* 2000).

Research indicates that the impact of maternal depression can be seen in children up to the age of four, even though the mother may no longer suffer from depression at that time (Logue 2001). Maternal depression that persists throughout the first twelve to fourteen months of a child's life may be linked to a child's behavioural problems and low cognitive ability during pre-school years. Children of depressed parents have been shown to be two to five times more likely to develop behaviour problems (Cummings *et al* 2000). They are also more likely to have problems relating to others, to have emotional and conduct disorders and to have problems with substance abuse in later life (Ross and Roberts 1999).

However, the link between parental depression and adverse child outcomes is by no means certain. There is evidence that successful treatment of depression can remove any adverse effects on a child's development. The research suggests that it is important to consider the impact of parents' emotional wellbeing on young children and that it is possible to ameliorate the worst impact of parental depression.

Fathers' involvement

While most research focuses on the mother-infant relationship, the father-infant relationship is often overlooked. Yet on average fathers now carry out one-third of parental childcare (EOC 2003). Fathers' and mothers' involvement with children has been found to be of a different nature, particularly when their children are young. Fathers are more likely to engage children in play activities while mothers tend to spend more time in routine caregiving activities (Parke 1996). Yet despite this, it is thought that mothers and fathers influence their children in similar ways with regard to the development of competence in social interactions, academic achievement and mental health (Lamb 1986). The gender of the parent is less important for child development than broader parenting style.

There is some evidence to suggest that the nature of the father-infant relationship in the first few months is important. Fathers who express positive attitudes about their three-month old babies are more likely to form secure attachments with their children as they grow older than fathers who do not. In turn, children with more secure parental attachments appear less likely to be socially isolated and aggressive later in childhood (Moore *et al* 1999).

Again, the first few months of life are likely to be important in establishing the style of parental relationship that can have a longer-term impact on child development. Studies of pre-schoolers have found that fathers providing as much as 40 per cent of their care demonstrate more cognitive competence, increased empathy and a greater sense of control over their surroundings (Kraemer 1995). Other research suggests it is the quality of the relationship between fathers and their children that matters more than the amount of time they spend together. Children with good relationships with their fathers have been reported to be more psychologically well-adjusted, to do better at school, to engage in less antisocial behaviour and to have more successful intimate adult relationships (Lamb 1996).

A number of studies have found that men take on greater roles in looking after children following their experience of taking parental leave (Moss and Devon 1999). One study of parental leave in Sweden found that men who took parental leave were twice as likely as other men to take equal responsibility for child care when their child was between two and three years old (Haas 1992).

Swedish evidence also suggests that those fathers who do not take parental leave may nevertheless be affected by its availability, the campaigns which promote it and the overall importance given to men looking after children. The time men spend caring for children in Sweden has increased over recent years, and the majority of fathers now report that (regardless of whether they take parental leave or not) they make adjustments to their work to accommodate their desire to play a greater role in childcare. About 60 per cent of Swedish fathers have reduced their work hours, turned down a promotion or avoided working overtime in order to be together with their children (Moss and Devon 1999).

There has been some research into the effects on fathers' relationships with their children according to whether they live with them or not. Unsurprisingly, there is likely to be less contact between fathers and their children when they do not live in the same household and this contact may diminish over time. Fathers who do not live with their children tend to be more involved when they live nearby, when they have a positive relationship with the child's mother as well as when they have financial resources and are in work (Burghes *et al* 1997). Yet while contact is obviously important, the evidence suggests that non-resident fathers' parenting styles are a more important predictor of good child outcomes than frequency of visits (EOC 2003).

Public policy has so far only played a limited role in encouraging and supporting paternal involvement during children's early years in general, including the first twelve months of life. Whilst limited, the evidence that is available suggests that the father-infant relationship is as important as the mother-infant relationship during this period.

The wider environment

It is difficult to isolate the impact that growing up in a particular environment has for child development over and above that of the immediate family. There is limited research in this area and what does exist largely relates to outcomes for older children. However, this research is useful in illuminating issues which may also be important during the first year of life.

For example, US research using data from the US National Longitudinal Survey of Youth (NLSY) and the Infant Health and Development Project (IHDP) found a strong and significant association between the presence of affluent families in a local neighbourhood and children's IQ scores at age three. The study pointed to the absence of relatively affluent families being important, rather than the presence of low-income families. There also appeared to be an association between the level of male joblessness and behavioural outcomes in young children.

The reason why these neighbourhood factors may have had an effect on children's outcomes is unclear. The study's authors suggest that the presence of affluent families could lead to better local services and community resources being provided, whilst the impact of male joblessness could be related to the type of role models available for children (Chase Lansdale *et al* 1997). However, much about the relationship between neighbourhoods and child development remains to be explored.

Better understood is the impact of care given by someone other than the primary caregiver on an infant's cognitive ability and behaviour in later life. A key concern has been whether entering childcare during the first year of life harms a child's ability to form secure attachments with adults. Some evidence suggests that childcare begun in the first year of life has a different effect on emotional adjustment and cognitive development than care begun later. Baydar and Brooks-Gunn (1991), for example, found that childcare during the first year of life has a negative effect for some groups, whilst care for children aged over one year has a positive effect. However, very few studies have controlled for the quality of childcare being provided. Those that do have found that it plays a vital role (NICHD 1997).

Recent studies have focused on the impact of the length of time young children spend in non-parental childcare. There have been some claims (notably by Jay Belsky) that longer experiences of childcare are associated with more aggressive behaviour among children. However other studies have demonstrated that spending many hours in non-parental care during this early period does not undermine children's healthy development. In fact, young children may benefit from opportunities to develop close relationships with different caregivers (Shonkoff and Phillips 2000).

The quality of childcare seems to be particularly important in relation to children from low income families. A comprehensive review of studies of childcare programmes across the developed world in the mid 1990s found that the quality of childcare exerted more influence on the development of children from low income families compared to other children.[1] For disadvantaged children, there was a greater positive impact as a result of high quality care and a greater negative impact from poor quality care (Boocock 1995). Other research supports this finding. For example, low income children's cognitive development has been found to benefit more from high quality child care compared to children from other families (Caughy et al 1994). This may be because the child care environment is more optimal (for example in terms of exposure to language) than the children's home environment.

Most of the evidence about the impact of the quality of childcare on later outcomes comes from the US. Although we can learn a great deal from carefully conducted research in other countries, there are important differences in the quality and type of care that is available in the UK.

Longitudinal research will be crucial if we are to fully understand the effects both of different types of childcare and the quality of childcare being provided on later outcomes in this country.

Conclusion

There is still much to learn both about the factors that are critical to child development during pregnancy and the first year of life and the way in which these factors have an impact. But the existing research tells us that the following issues are particularly important:

- Levels of income and material circumstances

- The quality of the parent-child interaction (both mother-child and father-child interaction)

- Mothers' physical health during pregnancy

- The emotional wellbeing of parents

- The wider environment (including the quality of childcare).

It is these critical factors that policy makers need to take into account when considering the support that is necessary during pregnancy and the first year of life. They also need to consider the balance of importance attached to these different factors. The harmful impacts of poverty, neglect, abuse and deprivation are well understood and protecting the health of mother and child has long been a public policy issue. But less acknowledged, in public policy terms at least, is the profound impact that the parent-child relationship has on an infant's development.

4. The impact of public policy

Parents and children can come into contact with a range of support and services during pregnancy and the first 12 months. However, there are some common elements to the support that is offered: antenatal and postnatal services (principally delivered by midwives and health visitors), financial support through the benefit system, and parenting and childcare services (both of which are underdeveloped). New approaches to the early years – Sure Start and the emergence of Early Excellence Centres (and in future 'children's centres') – are shaping the experience of families in some parts of the country, offering lessons as to how support might be developed in future.

In this chapter we look at antenatal, financial, parenting and childcare support to consider how they might achieve better – and more equal – outcomes for children.

Antenatal support

Throughout Europe routine antenatal care has long been considered an essential part of health services. The wide variety of provision in different countries does not allow for strong conclusions to be drawn about the link between types of antenatal support and different outcomes. However, there is some evidence that those countries with low perinatal mortality rates are more likely to have one dominant system separate from general health services, based on midwives providing care outside hospitals (Hemminki et al 2001). This evidence suggests that community midwifery services and the type of support being developed under Sure Start programmes are likely to be of particular benefit in terms of foetal and infant health.[2]

What is less clear is whether the UK's system of antenatal care offers the optimal level of support in terms of the frequency and timing of interventions. In the UK women are offered a relatively high number of antenatal visits. Most women attend around 13 antenatal visits, similar to women in Finland and Sweden (Lenton 2000). This is high by European standards. In France, for example, it is usual for women to attend seven antenatal visits.

However, attendance is much lower among certain groups. Antenatal visit attendance rates in England and Wales are much lower among Pakistani (24 per cent) and Bangladeshi (14 per cent) women, compared to white women (77 per cent), for example (Department of Health 1997). Other research suggests that there are insufficient numbers of antenatal classes to cater for all prospective parents in some parts of the country (Henricson *et al* 2001). Thus whilst antenatal services are widely provided, they are not universally experienced.

There is little clear evidence as to the importance of the frequency, timing or content of antenatal support, apart from the unsurprising finding that extremely poor antenatal care is associated with poor maternal and foetal outcomes (Delvaux and Buekens 1999). The need for more research in this area is clear, for example the Audit Commission has recommended controlled evaluations of antenatal services in the UK (Audit Commission 1999).

While it has been universally accepted that antenatal care is an important factor in determining the outcome of pregnancy for high-risk women, it is not necessarily the case that the current level of support is necessary for all pregnant women. Indeed there is concern that antenatal care may be over-utilised and some research has shown that reducing the number of antenatal visits may be clinically beneficial (McDuffie *et al* 1996). A World Health Organisation systematic review of randomised controlled trials of routine antenatal care concluded that the number of antenatal visits could be reduced in many developed countries without risk to mother or baby (Carroli *et al* 2001).

Twenty years ago the Royal College of Obstetricians and Gynaecologists recommended nine antenatal visits for first-time mothers and six visits for mothers of second and subsequent children (RCOG 1982). Other experts have made similar recommendations (US Department of Health and Human Service 1989). Reviewing the literature, Lenton (2000) concludes that the frequency of antenatal visits should be reduced to eight for low risk first-time mothers and six for low risk second and subsequent births with women who encounter problems between antenatal visits being able to access advice from midwives and primary care teams.

We know from research that early pregnancy is particularly important for certain health outcomes. It is known, for example, that the first trimester of pregnancy is a key period whereby a mother's nutrient intake can have an effect on an infant's birth weight (Doyle and Rees 2001). One study found that initiating antenatal care after the first trimester was associated with poor pregnancy outcomes (Gissler and Hemminki 1994). However, these findings are not universally supported (Thomas *et al* 1991). There is insufficient evidence to increase the number of antenatal interventions at this stage of pregnancy. Although some have advocated the development of pre-pregnancy care, there is little documented experience of its effectiveness (Czeizel 1999) and obvious difficulties of identifying a target group for support since between 30 and 50 per cent of pregnancies in England and Wales are unplanned (Maternity Alliance 2002a).

Aside from the frequency and timing of antenatal support, there is the question of the content of antenatal visits. Current antenatal care programmes in the UK originate from early 20th century models, which were largely focused on preventing maternal morbidity. The core of these models remains practically unchanged (Lenton 2000).

The importance of the antenatal period in terms of personal support and preparation for parenthood, as opposed to traditional antenatal healthcare, has been comparatively overlooked, despite demonstrations of the potency of even short periods of such support. Hodnett's (1998) review of the evidence found that women who received support from a trained person had shorter labours, less analgesia and operative delivery and their babies were in a better condition at birth. Some studies have reported the positive effects of home visiting during pregnancy. Elbourne *et al* found that women were more likely to be more content and less nervous at the birth and more likely to breastfeed (Elbourne et al 1989). The health effects of home visits are less certain, (Roberts 1997; Oakley 1992; Hodnett 1998), although one randomised controlled trial found that home visits by nurses during pregnancy was associated with reduced pregnancy-induced hypertension (Kitzman *et al* 1997).

There have long been calls for better information and support for parents not simply about the process of giving birth but also about motherhood, fatherhood and the social and emotional changes they are likely to face remains (Pugh and De'Ath 1984, Pugh *et al* 1994). There are a number of features which programmes for expectant parents might seek to address including: improving maternal education and diet, promoting potential parents' self-confidence and self-esteem, and building the skills required to promote key 'resilience' or protective factors in children.

While the UK has a well-developed system of antenatal support that undoubtedly makes a contribution to improving the wellbeing of expectant mothers and their infants, we know little about the exact value of different aspects of provision. The available research suggests that there is little need to increase the frequency of antenatal contact. Indeed, there may be grounds for decreasing contact, although this might have a damaging impact on parents' confidence and emotional wellbeing. What is not in doubt is the need to ensure that antenatal provision meets all the needs of expectant parents, by providing emotional support and preparation for parenthood, as well as routine advice about the process of giving birth.

Midwifery and health visiting support

Of all the professionals that work with families during pregnancy and the first year of a child's life, midwives and health visitors are the most important. This is partly because of the level of contact that they have with parents and children during the antenatal and postnatal period (midwives oversee 70% of births in the UK and health visitors aim to reach all families in the immediate postnatal period) but it is also because of the adaptable and empowering ways in which they can work.

Both midwives and health visitors are proactive in developing their work with families rather than having to be responsive to demands for care. Both groups of professionals also work in and outside the clinical setting, managing their work autonomously but in partnership with other professions. The health visiting service is predominately unsolicited and is not offered in relation to specific care needs, so it is able to respond to a range of service and community needs. Although there is some evidence that parents believe that health visitors' chief role is to police families (Foster 1988), in general both midwives and health visitors appear to be accepted by the community. They are allowed into people's homes without much hesitation as they command a relatively high level of public credibility and trust.

Midwifery and health visiting are closely allied to the nursing profession but at times have had difficulty sustaining their status in the medical world. Because of its complex history and roots in the public health field, health visiting has sometimes fallen foul of the medically-focused health service. Many health authorities reduced the number of health visitors in the 1990s in the belief that health visiting was not an effective service (particularly on grounds of cost) because of its primary focus on child health screening (Naish 2002). The continued dominance of acute care in health services has undermined the prospect of health visitors developing their wider public health role.

The midwifery and health visiting roles

Since the health visiting profession was founded there have been heated debates about its role and purpose. This has continued to the present day. In 1999, the current government rejected a recommendation that health visiting should be regarded as a specialist branch of nursing, instead reaffirming the statutory basis of health visiting as a separate profession. Nevertheless its place in the medical field is closely allied to the nursing profession, not least because since 1962 health visitors have been required to undergo nurse training before qualifying as health visitors.

Both midwifery and health visiting have a wide remit and a significant amount of autonomy to develop services to meet local needs. While midwives are required to provide medical advice and support during the antenatal period and supervise the birth, they can also offer a wide range of support in preparation for, and during, parenthood. The health visitor role is broader in that it can encompass the health and social wellbeing of the whole community (although with a particular focus on families with children under five). Health visitors can, for example, provide advice on employment and benefit rights, support fathers in their new role, give information on local support networks and advise on options for child care.

However, the wider roles of midwives and health visitors are often highly limited in practice. The support that is given in the antenatal and postnatal period largely focuses on routine physical examinations of mothers and babies rather than other dimensions of health such as the impact of having a baby on marital and family relationships. Much of the work involves routine child development assessments, increasingly coupled with the development of specialist health visiting services (for example in the field of infant mental health) (Salmon *et al* 2002). The need to move away from a routine assessment function to a wider public health role is being increasingly recognised with the acknowledgement that services often fail to give due importance to parent's emotional support and relationship needs (Singh and Newburn 2000; NCT 2000). The new competency framework agreed by the Nursing and Midwifery Council (implemented from September 2002) reaffirms the view that health visitors are expected to consider the parent's social and emotional wellbeing – taking account of the quality and nature of social support networks and the impact of the transition to parenthood.

However, in many parts of the country, social support still remains less of a priority. Naish (2002) argues that the work of midwives and health visitors should focus more on 'the spaces between parents and children, between parents themselves and between families and their wider communities'. In other words the practical and emotional support that families need in the few months following the birth of a child needs to be valued as much as work to support the healthy development of the newborn infant. This goes against the grain of the majority of health work, because of the lack of mainstream attention still given to tackling inequalities in health and the unwillingness to 'interfere' in family matters.

Yet the potential for achieving better outcomes for children and parents by offering emotional and social support remains. MacArthur *et al* (2002) tested the impact of extending midwifery support in this way in a randomised controlled trial and showed that, four months post childbirth, women's mental health measures were significantly better. Interestingly it was the content of the contact with mothers and children that changed rather than the number or duration of visits made. Other research has shown positive benefits of health visitors undertaking counselling interventions with mothers who are depressed (Acheson 1998) or with couples on the impact of having children on their relationships (Home Office 1998).

There would need to be changes to the way in which midwives and health visitors work if they are to provide greater socio-emotional support. Despite recent efforts, the nature of the client-professional role has rarely been characterised by partnership (Bidmead 2002). The earliest health visitors were employed to advise working class women on clean and hygienic living. The role was that of an expert trying to provide for the needs of the underprivileged. Changes to this approach were attempted during the 1970s. The 1976 Department of Health and Social Security report 'Fit for the Future' claimed: 'we believe that in our generation there is the opportunity to make the next essential step and to move to share responsibility.' Research during the 1980s and 1990s showed that health visitors were still not working in partnership with clients and favoured a top-down approach (Bidmead 2002). In their systematic review of health visiting Elkan *et al* (2000) have suggested that service managers may not construe partnership working as being 'real' work.

While health visitors have embraced many different styles of working, the profession is still too often characterised by professional dominance and control rather than by acting as an advocate for parents. The benefits of adopting a more empowering approach to supporting parents have been demonstrated (Barker 2002). In action research where health visitors have supported parents to identify solutions to their problems, improved outcomes for children and parents have been demonstrated. Some commentators have advocated the introduction of midwife assistants and community volunteers to work alongside health visitors and midwives to boost the practical and emotional support available to parents (Page 2002). This way of working is already being introduced in some Sure Start areas.

There appears to be particular value in encouraging peer support programmes to supplement the work of midwives and health visitors in relation to issues such as breastfeeding support. Despite considerable efforts to encourage breastfeeding in the UK, rates have remained static for the past 20 years with a strong disparity between social classes and ethnic groups. Just over half of new mothers from social class V make attempts to breastfeed compared to 90 per cent of new mothers from social class I. The decision to breastfeed seems to be influenced by practical knowledge and from seeing breastfeeding rather than by theoretical knowledge about its benefits (Hoddinott and Pill 1999). Peer-to-peer support with breastfeeding appears to be successful, possibly because it offers a more empowering approach to encouraging women to breastfeed.

Workforce issues

Current limitations in the scope of midwifery and health visiting services are in part due to capacity constraints. This may explain parents' varied experience of services across the country (Edwards 2002). There are currently around 18,000 midwives and 10,000 health visitors working in England (Department of Health 2002). These figures relate to the number of full-time equivalents and the number actually practising is greater since many work part-time. There are currently 33,000 practising midwives (Nursing and Midwifery Council 2002) and an estimated 20,000 practising health visitors.

Despite efforts to recruit to the professions, midwifery and health visiting both face staff shortages. The highest ever vacancy rates were recorded in the 2002 Royal College of Midwives annual staffing survey, throwing into doubt the likelihood of the Government reaching its target of recruiting 2,000 more midwives by 2004. The national midwifery vacancy rate is 2.8 per cent, with vacancy rates in London as high as seven per cent (Department of Health 2002). Similar vacancy rates are being experienced in the health visiting profession. As a result of these recruitment difficulties, many of those working in midwifery and health visiting are unable to fulfil their current roles let alone adopt new approaches and working practices; the sheer quantity of work they face means that they can not do more than provide a minimal service. There are reports of a reduction in the number of home visits undertaken by health visitors, with mothers being encouraged instead to attend clinics (Spooner 2001).

These problems are unlikely to abate in the near future. The midwifery and health visiting professions both have an ageing workforce. Around a third of health visitors and 20 per cent of midwives are over the age of 50 (Department of Health 2001; Nursing and Midwifery Council 2002). Almost all are women: only 0.2 per cent of midwives and 1.4 per cent of health visitors are men (Nursing and Midwifery Council 2002). The numbers of new entrants to the professions are not sufficient to replace those retiring, there are too few training places coming on stream, and there are fundamental concerns that levels of pay are insufficient to attract new people into the professions.

Co-ordination of services

Despite the fact that midwives and health visitors both work with parents and children[3] they rarely meet. They do not share a common identity and while they are working with identical population groups in practice they rarely exchange ideas and information about the population they work with and do not share a practice framework (Naish 2002).

The majority of midwives and health visitors have their caseloads organised by GP attachment, working to one or more GP practice, rather than on the basis of geographical area. This can create tensions with geographically defined services – such as those provided under the auspices of Sure Start. Where midwives and health visitors are being organised around geographical areas, there are more opportunities for cross-agency working, a reduction in duplication, high levels of knowledge about local issues and more effective community based support.

Both professions are largely self-managed and the lack of clarity of roles can lead to duplication of effort and gaps in services (Audit Commission 1994). Health visitors plan and deliver their work largely on their own. There is no infrastructure to support them in their work or help make decisions about where to focus. Some have suggested bringing midwifery and health visiting closer together under the remit of Primary Care Trusts' public health teams (Naish 2002).

Universal or targeted?

Health visitors offer a minimal universal service to all families with pre-school children. Every family with children under five has a named health visitor who can advise on child development and parenting issues such as teething, sleeping, feeding, immunisation and any special needs.

Yet in practice, few families have more than very occasional contact with a health visitor. There is also evidence which suggests that parents who are more likely to be in need can be less likely to receive a home visit or attend a clinic (Audit Commission 1994).

There has never been a serious attempt to redistribute health care resources and health workers towards greatest need, according to social deprivation or other measures. The Government has already proposed distributing resources to the most deprived areas by giving community practitioners and health visitors their own community budgets to spend on improving health outcomes in the poorest communities, although the budgets are tiny at £5,000 a year. Some have called for the health visitor and midwifery workforce to be distributed according to measures of social deprivation indices as a proxy for need for health care – not simply on the basis of population size (Naish 2002).

The benefits of providing a universal service are that it is non-stigmatising and best able to achieve early intervention. However, it may be possible to supplement this provision with more effective targeting of additional resources. This is the direction in which health visiting is already heading. It is increasingly recognised that universal health care for young children may need to be defined in a new way (see for example Hall 2001). The universal points of contact with the health service during pregnancy and the first year of life should be fully examined to see whether there is a case for reducing some face-to-face contact in order to redirect resources on targeted interventions.

The work of midwives and health visitors is a crucial component of the support given to parents and children. There are strong grounds for reforming these roles so they meet a wider range of parents' needs, particularly providing emotional and social support in the early months following birth. Such a transformation will involve considerable challenges. Capacity problems due to workforce shortages remain a significant barrier to change. As well as measures to tackle these problems, the balance of the universal and targeted work of midwives and health visitors needs to be carefully considered. Even with these changes, it is likely that the increase in social and emotional support that parents need during pregnancy and the first few months of an infant's life will not be met by these professionals alone.

Parenting support

There is now a variety of different parenting programmes available in the UK, including parenting education projects, counselling and therapy services, self-help groups and information services. Services are provided by health professionals, social workers and independent counsellors, as well as the voluntary sector.

However, the evidence suggests that services fall well short of providing universal support. One survey found that just under half of parents did not know where to go to get advice and help for family problems (MORI 1999). Substantial gaps in provision have been identified. Henricson et al (2001) found that early preventative services are in short supply and that some services are having to forgo their preventative function to meet gaps in specialist and crisis intervention. Particular gaps include support for minority ethnic families and (all) fathers, as well as support for families with disabled children, for teenage parents and for families with experience of mental health problems. Relationship support services are very poorly developed. The Lord Chancellor's Department has acknowledged that pregnancy and the birth of a child is a key transition point when relationship support can be beneficial stressing that all those who have contact with parents in the postnatal period (including health visitors) must sufficient training to identify and help with couple's emotional problems (Lord Chancellor's Department 2002).

As well as gaps in the content of support that is available to parents, many services also fail to fit in with modern family life. A recent survey showed that a quarter of mothers and 45 per cent of fathers regularly work in the evening and 38 per cent of mothers work at least one Saturday a month (La Valle *et al* 2002). The challenge for policy makers and practitioners is therefore not only to provide the right type of support to parents, but in ways which fit in with the lifestyles of today's families.

Developing effective programmes to support good parenting has proved problematic because it has been difficult to determine what is required to alter parenting behaviour (Shonkoff and Phillips 2000). In addition, almost all existing evaluations of parenting support relate to work with older children; there is not a substantial body of evidence evaluating parenting support in the early months.

There is, however, evidence of the effectiveness of programmes targeted at infants among high-risk populations (see for example Avon Premature Infant Project 1998; Aronen and Kurkela 1996). This suggests that where developmental or social support is given to families of pre-term children (children born at 32 weeks gestation or less) during the first two years of life, small, but significant improvements in child development can be detected (Avon Premature Infant Project 1998). Parent advisor schemes produce a similar effect as developmentally focused interventions, suggesting the effect may be the result of improving maternal confidence, wellbeing and self-esteem.

Similar evidence has been found in relation to older children. Controlled trials (Webster-Stratton *et al* 1989; Sanders *et al* 2000) and systematic reviews (Barlow and Coren 2000) have shown that it is possible to influence parenting in ways which are beneficial to the emotional and social development of children and the mental health of parents. Parenting programmes have been shown to improve maternal psychosocial health (Barlow and Coren 2000; Patterson *et al* 2002) relationships (Grimshaw and McGuire 1998), and reduce child behaviour problems (Patterson *et al* 2001; Scott *et al* 2001).

Evaluations of successful parenting programmes have shown that the best outcomes seem to be associated with the availability of regular support focused on the whole needs of the family and based in the community, accompanied by additional intervention for high-risk groups. The most effective programmes tend to start early, preferably during pregnancy, are continuous, occur with some intensity, take account of multiple factors, develop an appropriate alliance with parents, target the most needy, relate help to need, are home based and use well trained and supported staff. Although long-term programmes (lasting one to five years or more) can be effective, particularly for promoting cognitive and academic progress, the evidence is less clear in terms of mental health outcomes (Mental Health Foundation 2002).

Centre-based support

Centre-based (as opposed to home-based) educational interventions for older children are associated with improved cognitive and language development and subsequent school achievement (Mental Health Foundation 2002). Group based programmes have been shown to be both effective and cost-effective: community-based parent training schemes may be up to six times as cost effective as individual clinic-based programmes (Barlow 1999).

Parents have strong views about the nature of the support they would like to receive. Studies show parents feel there is insufficient information about what it is like to become a parent, too little advice about the 'pitfalls' that might be experienced and insufficient sources of immediate help and advice if they need reassurance and guidance (Curtice 1989; McCormick 2001).

When asked about their preparedness for parenthood, parents openly express uncertainty about how to approach certain tasks and say that they would welcome practical help and guidance on the basics of caring for a baby (such as feeding, bathing, sleep and feeding patterns, breastfeeding and changing nappies). Parents also request more help with child development issues and in particular want to know more about the role they can play in developing the emotional, social and cognitive skills of their babies (Edwards 2002).

Yet little time is devoted to helping new parents in learning to undertake these new tasks. Parents say that the support offered to them after the birth of a child can often be child-focused and insufficiently family-focused (Moorman and Ball 2001). Fathers feel particularly under-supported in the parenting role; they report feeling sidelined at clinic appointments, not being allowed to stay with their partner in hospital after the birth (outside of visiting hours) and feeling unable to ask questions or to get time off to attend antenatal appointments (Edwards 2002).

Parents say they want to be acknowledged as experts in their own lives, active agents who must be listened to and involved with planning services, rather than passive recipients of advice (Ghate and Hazel 2002). They often express the need simply to talk over issues of concern with someone (Cragg et al 2002). Continuity of support for parents is also important. One study of thirty families where there was concern about a baby's growth and development found that parents wanted to be able to build a relationship with one professional over a period of time rather than see different people and have to repeat questions to different professionals (Underdown 2000). Some parents welcome the idea of there being more support in the home in the weeks after having a baby (Edwards 2002).

Parents seem to value the help, support, advice and feedback they get from non-experts, including their peers (Pugh et al 1994). Qualitative research conducted with expectant mothers and mothers with young babies in Scotland found that mothers favoured advice and support from other women who were pregnant or already had children, rather than professional sources, with most women welcoming more opportunities to meet other women in a similar situation (McCormick 2001). Some studies have found no difference in outcomes between a well trained lay home visitor and an MSc level professional. Others question whether such workers are able to influence parenting behaviours arguing that their greatest strength instead lies in improving mothers' emotional wellbeing (Mental Health Foundation 2002). Nevertheless, the impact of volunteer-based programmes such as Home-Start have been shown to be beneficial, and non-directive support provided by lay workers has been shown to have a positive impact on child development for at-risk populations (Buchan *et al* 1998; Davis and Ali Choudry 1987).

Home-visiting schemes

Home-visiting is now a common feature of Sure Start programmes, with most programmes offering at least one routine home visit per child under the age of one, with additional (but not necessarily universal) home visiting support available.

Studies have shown that home-visiting schemes undertaken in infancy are associated with fewer problems among adolescents (Aronen and Kurkela 1996). They have also been shown to be successful in reducing child abuse and neglect and improving maternal mental health (Gomby *et al* 1999; Olds *et al* 1997). A 15-year follow up of a randomised controlled trial in the US found that those who had received home visits had fewer behavioural problems associated with the use of alcohol and other drugs, received welfare support for a shorter period and had fewer arrests (Olds *et al* 1997). However, home visiting programmes are not always associated with significant improvements in child development or child outcomes (Gomby *et al* 1999).

There is some evidence that home-visiting by lay people during children's early years, if well-designed, of adequate intensity and duration and carried out by carefully selected, trained and supervised home visitors, can have positive short- and long-term effects. For example, a systematic review also found that programmes of home visits by professional or specially trained lay care givers tended to be associated with decreased rates of childhood injury (Hodnett and Roberts 1998).

In the UK most evidence of the impact of home visiting by lay people comes from evaluations of Home-Start projects. Home-Start is a voluntary organisation that offers support and practical help to young families under stress in their own homes, in an attempt to prevent family crisis and breakdown. Where Home-Start projects work successfully they bridge the gap between a universal service provided by health visitors and targeted services provided by social services. Schemes employ organisers, supported by administrative assistants, who recruit, train and support volunteers, usually mothers themselves, who offer support to mothers with children under five. Other similar voluntary schemes exist in the UK, including Newpin, a voluntary group that provides support to parents under stress.

The majority of families supported by Home-Start schemes are economically vulnerable, lone parents, living in rented accommodation and suffering from high levels of ill health. In as many as one in ten families participating in the scheme in some areas there had been or were child protection concerns (Frost *et al* 2000). Since it is a voluntary scheme Home-Start is widely seen to be non-stigmatising and trusted. However, there is some evidence that support is not always welcomed and intervention can sometimes be seen as stigmatising (Frost *et al* 2000).

Evaluations have demonstrated that access to Home-Start may improve emotional wellbeing in around one in two cases. The aspects of the service that are seen by parents to be important are receiving regular support from someone who listens, improving informal networks of support and having another source of support when the help from a health visitor ends. There is evidence that parents find it important to have someone with whom they can share feelings, who is non-judgmental, shows concern and in whom they can confide. Around half of families participating in Home-Start schemes show improvements in their parenting skills (Frost *et al* 2000).

Despite evidence of the beneficial impact of centre and home-based parenting support, its impact may not be sustained. Parents can have difficulties gaining the support of partners in implementing the techniques learned, changing their established habits and those of their partners, finding time to parent together and incorporating the techniques into their already busy lives. In addition most programmes have an attrition effect: between 20 per cent and 67 per cent of families leave home-visiting programmes without completing them (Gomby 1999). This means that evaluations of parenting programmes may over-estimate the beneficial impact. In addition, since many of the existing parenting programmes are locally based, the extent to which their success can be replicated in national programmes must be considered.

Understanding the exact nature of the benefits of providing parental support (particularly in relation to parents of younger children) remains difficult, particularly because of the scarcity of evidence. The studies that have been undertaken have mainly taken place in health settings and with high-risk populations; their findings may not be applicable across the population as a whole. Nevertheless the evidence is sufficient to suggest ways in which support for parents with young children could be enhanced and where significant gaps in provision still need to be filled. The success of both group-based parenting programmes and individual home-based support suggest that a range of services would be beneficial.

Childcare

For many children, the quality of the non-parental childcare they receive in the first year of life will be an important factor in their development. Two thirds of mothers taking maternity leave from paid employment return to work within 10 months of the birth. The majority of families rely on relatives for childcare support, but formal childcare outside the family home is now an important reality for many.

The introduction of the national childcare strategy in 1998 placed childcare higher on the political agenda than ever before. Considerable investment has since gone into improving the UK's level of childcare provision, traditionally one of the least developed in Europe.

Overall, change in childcare policy has come faster than change in practice. By 2001 there was one registered childcare place per seven children under eight years of age, compared to one per nine children in 1997. The Government aims to create 1.6 million new childcare places by 2004.

For younger children the level of childcare provision remains limited. Care in the home of the parent or carer is the most common form of formal care for children under the age of one with registered childminders or unregistered nannies. The number of childminders has actually decreased in recent years, a trend exacerbated by problems with the registration process. Despite a government recruitment campaign, there remain significant problems recruiting childcare workers.

Where good quality group-based care has been developed – such as in a number of Early Excellence Centres – it can provide an environment in which children can thrive. Yet nursery-based care for under ones is limited and can be very expensive. Overall British parents typically pay £6,650 per year for childcare for a child under two (Daycare Trust 2003). Help with costs via the childcare tax credit, while more generous than its predecessor, does not meet full childcare costs and only those who are in employment for more than 16 hours a week are eligible for support. Families with more than two children get no extra help with childcare costs, exacerbating the difference in financial support between smaller and larger families.

Improving the quality of childcare services remains an objective of government. All registered childcare provision is now inspected by OFSTED. In addition the first major UK study on the effectiveness of early years' education (the Effective Provision of Pre-School Education project) is underway. This will provide much-needed evidence of the contribution that different forms of pre-school provision in the UK (as well as the home environment) can make in terms of children's development.

In July 2002 the Government announced details of a new integrated budget for childcare and early years learning worth £1.5 billion a year by 2005/6. The Government also announced the creation of children's centres in disadvantaged areas, where possible building on Sure Start provision and other existing facilities, but going on to provide services for an additional 300,000 children by 2005-6. Funding for childcare is set to more than double in real terms between 2002-03 and 2005-6.

There are many opportunities to develop support for parents and children under the umbrella of Sure Start. However, the reach of Sure Start initiatives remains limited. 520 local programmes will be established in the poorest areas of the UK by 2003/4, but this will only cover an estimated one-third of children under four living in poverty. One option would be to extend Sure Start to all geographic areas, something that would require a very high level of public investment. Another would be to seek to 'mainstream' the Sure Start approach across different public services. There is currently much debate about which of these approaches, or some combination of the two, is more appropriate.

However, an equally substantial challenge remains on the policy horizon: that of increasing the availability of good quality childcare provision required for young children to a level that is more in keeping with the needs of modern families. Despite high demand, the childcare market is not delivering nearly the amount of good quality, affordable childcare required. Without a substantial growth in provision, only a small – and privileged – minority will benefit from the experience of good quality early years' provision.

Financial support

When asked about the kind of support that they would want government to provide, parents are most likely to cite the need for greater financial support. Practical support in the form of cash benefits, childcare places or paid parental leave are often considered more obvious interventions for government than guidance on parenting, healthy eating or parent-child interaction (Edwards 2002).

The financial support available for parents has altered substantially in the last 50 years and now consists of a complex mix of means-tested and non-means-tested support, both in cash and in kind (Bennett 2002). In the past the UK has had comparatively low levels of financial support for parents. There has also been a significant financial penalty attached to motherhood, compared with many other industrialised countries. However, a number of changes in financial support have been introduced in recent years.

In 1999 the Prime Minister set the ambitious target of eliminating child poverty within a generation. Young children have become a particular focus of government policy and, following the publication of research revealing that parents spent roughly the same on younger as on older children (Middleton *et al* 1997), were the subject of benefit improvements from the 1999 Budget onwards. By October 2002, income support rates for younger children had nearly doubled in real terms since 1997. A new 'baby tax credit' was introduced in April 2002. This provides an extra payment on top of the children's tax credit for the first year of a baby's life. In addition. a new Child Trust Fund is being introduced. This will provide a universal endowment for all babies with a higher endowment for poorer families.

Changes have also been made in relation to maternity, paternity and parental leave. Maternity leave with pay has been extended (from April 2003) to 26 weeks, with a further 26 weeks of unpaid leave, and the qualifying service period has been reduced. Instead of having to take 11 weeks of maternity leave prior to the birth or losing it, women can now choose when to start their leave.

The UK now has the longest maternity leave in Europe but half of the leave entitlement is unpaid and the remainder is paid at a relatively low level of income replacement (90 per cent of earnings for six weeks plus 20 weeks at £100 from April 2003). There is some additional support for those who are not eligible for statutory maternity pay and a lump sum maternity grant is available for some groups on low incomes. The Sure Start Maternity Grant was introduced in 2000 to replace the maternity payment from the Social Fund. The grant was increased in stages, and is now worth £500 and is conditional on contact with a health professional. Despite these recent improvements, the fact that most of the maternity leave entitlement is either unpaid or paid at a low flat-rate means that the overall the financial support for maternity is low by European standards.

Unpaid time off for (emergency) family reasons was introduced in December 1999 with no qualifying service. Each parent of a child under 16 can take up to ten days per year. Parental leave was introduced at the same time and is also unpaid. Leave can be taken for up to 13 weeks in total, available to each parent of children under six (or older for disabled children), as long as they have completed one year's qualifying service. Up to four weeks can be taken in any one year, in blocks of one or more complete week(s) at a time, although this may be able to be changed in negotiation with the employer. Employers can defer the leave for business reasons, and there has been no real attempt to encourage fathers to make use of it.

Take up of parental leave has so far been lower than expected. Survey evidence collected by the Department for Trade and Industry in autumn 2000 found that 3 per cent of employed parents had taken parental leave – lower than the 10 per cent of fathers and 50 per cent of mothers who had originally been estimated to take leave. Interestingly, take-up rates for mothers and fathers were identical, although a gender difference may have been obscured by the overall low take-up rate. The DTI has since lowered its estimate of take up to 3-12 per cent.

From April 2003 fathers are entitled to two weeks paternity leave paid at the same rate as flat-rate statutory maternity pay. Fathers can take the leave at any time in the first eight weeks following the birth of their child. The Government is currently considering whether to extend the period of paid paternity leave or introduce additional unpaid leave (HM Treasury/DTI 2003).

Reform of in-kind support for low-income families is currently under consultation in the UK. The Welfare Foods Scheme was established over 60 years ago and provides tokens for milk (both in liquid form and as infant formula) and vitamins to expectant and nursing mothers, and to infants and children under 5. It also provides milk to those in day care and for a very few disabled children. Eligibility is restricted to those on low incomes (those receiving income support and working families tax credit). Around 55,000 pregnant women and 808,000 mothers and children in England, Scotland and Wales benefit from the scheme.

Several problems with the scheme – in particular the perception that it offers a disincentive to mothers to breastfeed, and the fact that the scheme does not meet the wider nutritional needs of pregnant women and young children – have led the Government to review it (Department of Health 2002). It is proposed that a new scheme – Healthy Start – should be launched in 2004. This scheme will include a broader range of foods such as fruit and vegetables, cereal-based food and other foods suitable for weaning. A fixed value voucher will be introduced, instead of the present token, to enable pregnant women and mothers to buy a wider range of foods broadly equivalent to the value of seven pints of liquid milk (vitamins would be delivered separately). Healthy Start will be used to build better links between the NHS and the mothers and children who will be covered by the scheme, aligning more closely the arrangements for pregnant women between Healthy Start and the Sure Start Maternity Grant. Mothers-to-be will register for Healthy Start by attending an early antenatal booking visit for health advice. Registration will be renewed at a child health clinic within three months of the birth and through clinic attendance at twelve to fourteen months.

Such a rapid period of policy development is likely to result in improvements for families with children. A recent analysis of the 'child benefit package' of financial support for children in 22 countries at July 2001 found a significant improvement in the UK's relative position compared to a similar cross-national comparison in 1992 (although these figures are not broken down by age group) (Bradshaw and Finch 2002). In 2000/01 about half a million fewer children were living in low-income households compared to 1996/7. The Government may well meet its interim pledge to cut child poverty by a quarter between 1998/9 and 2004/5, although some have argued that further measures will be needed even to achieve this (Piachaud and Sutherland 2002).

However, there remain concerns about the likelihood of reducing child poverty to acceptable levels. Child poverty rates in the UK remain among the highest level in the European Union. Despite substantial improvements to benefits, child poverty rates have not fallen rapidly.

Both employment rates among families with children and benefit rates would need to rise substantially to eradicate child poverty. This is partly because of the difficulty of reducing relative poverty in the face of persistent (and rising) income inequality.

There also remain some notable gaps in financial provision, with some groups left out or left behind (Bennett 2002). In 1999/2000, 52 per cent of mothers having children received neither statutory maternity allowance (though more would qualify now).[4] Poverty rates are also particularly high among lone parent families and those living in large families. In addition there is concern that current poverty rates may underestimate the level of poverty among young children because the McClements equivalence scale used to calculate the official poverty statistics gives a low value to young children (Bennett 2002).

Despite considerable improvements to financial support for families with children, substantial further changes will be required to protect families from poverty. The availability of improved leave arrangements is undermined by the low or unpaid nature of the financial support that accompanies them. And despite the case being made for years by maternity groups and others there have been no moves to improve financial support for those on low incomes during pregnancy.

Conclusion

It is vital that the Government redoubles its efforts to lift families out of poverty. At the same time, it must also begin to address a significant gap in provision during pregnancy and the first year of life – that of improving the emotional and social support available to parents. This gap needs to be tackled at every major stage of public policy intervention in the antenatal and postnatal period, through the work of midwives and health visitors, parenting schemes, childcare and home visiting programmes. The success of lay worker and peer-to-peer parenting schemes suggests that additional support can be delivered by non-professionals. Supplementary support of this kind may also help deliver the level of services required to ensure that there is base-line universal access to parenting support, onto which additional targeted help can then be added.

5. Improving support for parents and children

Despite a strong commitment to tackling child poverty and improving support for parents and children, the current Government has never been entirely comfortable with articulating an explicit commitment to reducing inequality, nor has it found its voice on the role of public policy in relation to family life.

New Labour has not shied away from a policy of redistribution in order to improve the living standards of poor families, but neither has it trumpeted one. Increases to benefits, new tax credits and the introduction of the new Child Trust Fund (or 'baby bond') have meant that low-income families have received the lion's share of improvements in financial support. Yet despite the Government's pledge to eradicate child poverty within a generation, such changes have generally been introduced without much fanfare.

What is more, quiet redistribution has yet to produce the outcomes the Government hoped for. Although benefit and tax credit levels have increased and absolute living standards among poor families have generally improved, relative poverty rates remain high and the gap between rich and poor in Britain has hardly changed.

In this context the Government has been coy about being seen to adopt an explicit agenda in pursuit of greater income equality. Beyond continuing to pursue its redistributive tax credit and benefit strategy, it has not indicated that it is willing to go further, to address the kinds of issues that would need to be tackled if inequality was to decrease. Income and inheritance tax reform, for example, has yet to feature on the policy-making agenda.

Having not sought out public support for the tax credit and benefit strategy, the prospect of convincing the public of the need for more radical changes has inevitably been reduced. On the basis of current plans, the inequalities that emerge soon after birth are unlikely to be significantly reduced. For that to be possible, the Government would first need to convince the electorate of the importance of a more ambitious approach towards tackling inequalities, including during the early years.

It is also clear that a bolder income strategy would not be enough to achieve greater equality in life chances. In the past public policy has paid too little attention to the impact that the social and familial context has on a child's development. A strategy that focuses solely on money as the means to reduce inequality will fail.

The question of the appropriateness of the State's involvement in family life has long been debated. Historically it has been the Right with the stronger story to tell. It has argued that government policies have systematically undermined the institution of marriage, which in turn has led to family breakdown with consequential problems for society. The Right has sought to convey family support as an infringement of individual liberty:

> The family's most dangerous enemies may not turn out to be those who have openly declared war...It is less easy to fight against the armies of those who are 'only here to help' – those who claim to come with the best intentions but come armed, all the same, with statutory powers and administrative instruments....What is objectionable is not merely that these public officials are frequently wrong – though they are. Nor is it for the most part that we have no means of controlling or challenging their activities – though that is often true too. What is always affronting, offensive and distressing is the simple fact of their intrusion into our private space. (Mount 1982)

Such exaggerated concerns about the infringement of personal liberty have not been met by an equally robust retort from the Left. The Government has claimed that is has tried to pursue a family policy which is 'neither a 'back to basics' fundamentalism, trying to turn back the clock, nor an 'anything goes' liberalism which denies the fact that how families behave affects us all' (Home Office 1998). But the consequence has been continued uncertainty about the extent to which public policy should become involved in family life.

The political enthusiasm to embrace a more preventative and proactive approach to family support, witnessed at the time the National Family and Parenting Institute was established by the Government, appears to have waned. A consultation paper on the Family, published in 1998, was followed by an apparent loss of confidence within government about its own position. No White Paper emerged and specific policy proposals were shelved.

As a consequence a notable gap in family policy has occurred whereby family support as it relates to 'failing' families has had greater prominence in the Government's agenda than support for all families with children. Policy makers are more confident of the legitimacy of the State's involvement in family life in such circumstances. Yet this emphasis on 'failing' families has served to reinforce a message that family support is about instructing and changing poor behaviour and consequently it is often perceived to be intrusive and unwelcome.

Unsurprisingly the notion of government intervention to develop parenting skills is not automatically welcomed by parents (Edwards 2002). The National Family and Parenting Institute notes that 'there are anxieties over how intrusive the state should be and the degree to which parenting may become 'professionalised' by too great a focus on social support.' (Henricson *et al* 2001). In a recent study over half of parents of 8-12 year old children surveyed said that they did not feel parents needed professional advice and guidance to help them bring up children (Gillies and Edwards 2003). For the Government to be able to provide greater support to parents with their parenting role – support which appears to be critical to improving children's development – it must first convince parents of the legitimacy of the State's involvement in family life.

Part of the answer must be a greater acknowledgement of the range of factors that have an impact on children's development, and increased efforts by government to approach policy in a more joined-up way. There is now greater prospect of the Government achieving this goal. The establishment of the Children and Young People's Unit (with a cross-government remit but based within the Department for Education and Skills) and the new integrated budget for childcare and early years' education offer the opportunity for more joined-up policy development. The national framework documents (such as the Department of Health's forthcoming National Service Frameworks for Children, the Home Office's National Framework for Parenting Support, and the Department for Education and Skills' Framework for Effective Practice for practitioners working with children under 3s) similarly promise a more co-ordinated approach to policy-making.

The introduction of Sure Start in some areas of the country also provides a basis on which to build greater acceptance of the value of parenting support. In offering universal support in certain (geographically defined) populations, Sure Start now provides a framework for a wide range of services that are flexible, community based and centred on the needs of parents and children. This different approach to public policy making has resulted in a bottom-up, non-uniform, universal set of services and a new focus to the kind of support offered to parents and children; the recognition that parents require emotional and practical support, as well as health advice and financial support. It provides a solid foundation on which future services could be built.

The combination of the Government's timidity in tackling inequality and a continued reticence about being seen to cross the threshold into the private world of the family is constraining progress on achieving more equal life chances for children. Both pose considerable challenges politically; but they are both crucial to achieving change.

Universal or targeted?

Traditional health support for children and families in the early months of life is universally provided, with targeted interventions for at risk populations. Sure Start follows in the same tradition, albeit on a geographical basis. Given that as many as one in three first time parents report feeling unprepared for parenthood, with middle-class parents, those on low incomes and single parents all equally ill-prepared (Home Start 2000), the value of providing universal support during this period is clear.

Despite the fact that most parenting programmes focus on parents of children who already have behavioural problems, there are some studies (albeit involving older children) that have demonstrated the effectiveness of open access services in preventing problems emerging (Webster-Stratton and Hammond 1997). Interest in attending a parenting programme is not related to social-class but can be better predicted by the existence of behaviour problems in children. Although children from deprived backgrounds are one and a half times as likely to suffer from behaviour problems as children from non-deprived backgrounds, research suggests that the use of a selective approach of support would miss two-fifths of children with problems (Patterson *et al* 2002).

As this report has already outlined, the extent to which universal health service support should be complemented by targeted interventions is a live debate (Hall 2001). Given the current demands on public services there is a clear need to ensure that midwifery and health visiting services are able to respond to the greatest needs in local communities while at the same time retaining a meaningful (but reduced) level of contact with all families. Enhanced levels of social and emotional support for parents cannot be provided by these professionals alone. The Government should aspire to be able to offer a universal guarantee of some form of parenting support but this could only be met with the help of a wide range of professional and lay- run community services.

Early preparation for parenthood

Given that prospective mothers in the UK are offered a greater number of antenatal visits than in many other countries, and the fact that there is no evidence of any risk associated with having fewer visits, there might be a case for reducing the number of appointments in the antenatal period.

However, two factors would need to be taken into account. Firstly parents tend to report that they received the right amount of antenatal appointments and do not support the suggestion that they should be reduced (Edwards 2002). Even if there was no greater clinical risk of reducing the number of antenatal visits, the psychological impact of reducing support in this period may be undesirable. Secondly, it is clear that not all prospective parents attend antenatal visits, particularly those that are most at risk.

Given the comparative lack of emotional and practical preparation for parenthood in the antenatal period, increasing the amount of parent preparation support but keeping the same number of antenatal visits appears a more preferable approach. However, in general there is a need for much more rigorous evaluation of antenatal services. For example, home-visiting antenatal support should be more widely piloted and evaluated.

Transforming the health visiting and midwifery roles

Given current recruitment difficulties, the future of health visiting and midwifery lies primarily in finding ways to renew an ageing and declining workforce. The need for better workforce planning and a strengthened recruitment drive is evident. However, more fundamental change may be needed if a younger generation of health visitors and midwives is to be attracted into the professions. One option that should be considered would be to allow direct entry into training for health visitors, returning to the pre-1962 position whereby health visitors did not need to be qualified as a nurse before undertaking training.

If midwives and health visitors are to be able to provide the social and emotional support to parents that research indicates is vital for child development (and which many practitioners themselves want to provide), the nature of their role will need to change. It will need to move away from a child health monitoring approach to a more rounded role in supporting families; a move that is already taking place as the profession enhances its public health role.

This would require greater emphasis on the role that health visitors and midwives play in supporting adults in preparation for, and support during, parenthood. Midwives and health visitors should provide greater emotional and social support to both fathers and mothers in the first months following the birth of a child and health visitors should have more contact with parents prior to the birth. To avoid such an approach being seen as judgmental or 'policing', health visitors and midwives will need to strengthen the ways in which they work in partnership with communities, and with fathers as well as mothers. Such skills will need to be given more emphasis in midwifery and health visitor training. Arguably moves towards working in partnership with parents might be undermined if professionals are given a greater role as gatekeepers for welfare benefits, as is being suggested under the Government's proposals to reform the Welfare Foods Scheme.

Given the current shortage of health visitors and midwives, any broadening of their role at this time will be difficult to deliver. This brings into question the nature of the universal service that midwives and health visitors can realistically provide. There is a case for better targeting of resources to areas of high deprivation with the health visitor and midwifery workforce distributed according to measures of social deprivation indices as a proxy for need for health care – not simply on the basis of population size. This suggests that in future, the universal support that health visitors provide in the postnatal period will need to be supplemented with additional non-professional support.

Home Visitors: a new type of service

In additional to enhancing the social and emotional support provided to parents by midwives and health visitors, and by parenting groups or classes, a new service to provide practical and emotional support for parents should now be explored. The service would consist of an 'on your side' advocate and mentor for parents, someone who would be able to provide regular and continuous support from the third trimester of pregnancy, during the early months of a child's life and potentially throughout the first year.

A Home Visitor could be an experienced parent or grandparent or someone who has trained as a midwife or health visitor. They would take on a different role to health professionals in acting as a mentor and personal adviser – providing a gateway to a range of services for parents. They would be active in the community in helping develop services to meet parents' needs.

The idea of a home visitor was supported by parents interviewed in IPPR's qualitative research (Edwards 2002). Parents are drawn to the notion of a support person who is also an experienced parent and liked the idea of being in touch with someone slightly removed from mainstream public services. Such support could be directed at fathers as well as mothers. The relationship between a home visitor and parents would be less formal than might be possible to achieve by those working in a professional capacity with parents. Parents sometimes describe how they are unable to be frank about their own experiences (such as post natal depression and not forming an immediate bond with their baby), and claim that they feel that they have to put on a 'front' for the midwife or health visitor. They say they might find a home visitor easier to talk to.

Parents raise some qualifications about the role of a 'lay' home visitor (Edwards 2002). Parents would want to get to know the home visitor during pregnancy rather than meet them for the first time after the birth, in order to build trust and confidence in the relationship. Some (although relatively few) felt that this role was already filled by their health visitor. Others said they were confident in seeking information and advice themselves, and wouldn't necessarily want another layer of visits imposed. Not all wanted the visitor to be a 'home' visitor, saying they would be more comfortable visiting this 'on your side' advocate in another setting, or contacting them by phone. Among the least confident mothers (often also the youngest) the idea of seeking outside support, even in this more informal format, was not welcomed. There is a real challenge in getting support services to those most in need in a way they feel comfortable with.

Such concerns would need to be taken into account in developing new services. Lessons from existing projects would also need to be learnt, since there are already many successful volunteer and/or peer initiatives on which the home visitor role could be based. Schemes that have been shown to be successful in providing practical and emotional support to parents include Home-Start, 'community mother' schemes and para-professionals working in Sure Start areas. Many Sure Start programmes are already employing non-clinical staff to visit families at home to provide information about services, to undertake practical tasks, to support breastfeeding, to accompany group activities and other social support and to provide continuity between midwifery and health visiting services. Local mothers have been trained in these roles.

Responses to the National Family and Parenting Institute consultation on developing family support suggested the introduction of community volunteers to boost practical and emotional support to parents before and after the birth of a child would be welcome (Page 2002). Development of a home visitor role could also complement the emergence of new roles in health and social care (Kendall and Harker 2002). This would be in keeping with the desire to evolve multi-professional local networks of parenting support, involving parents and others in the community in the design and delivery of services (Wolfendale and Einzig 1999). Funding to encourage the development of Home Visitor support could be ring-fenced as part of the Government's plans for a £25 million parenting fund, as announced in the 2002 Spending Review.

A Home Visitor Service would:

- Offer practical and emotional support to mothers and fathers in their home from the third trimester to the early months and potentially throughout the first year
- Offer 'on your side' support for parents
- Be delivered by experienced parents, grandparents or those who have previously trained as a midwife or health visitor but are no longer working in that role
- Build on existing provision in Sure Start areas and in areas where home-visiting schemes are being run by voluntary organisations
- Direct parents to other services in the community and represent parents' views and needs in shaping the development of local services
- Develop in response to individual and local community needs, rather than adopting a 'one size fits all' model
- Be developed through funding from the Parenting Fund

Children's Centres

The Government has announced the intention to introduce children's centres in some of the most deprived areas in the country. Along with a range of services for children and parents, these centres will provide the focus for good quality childcare services in a locality.

Children's centres could provide a one-stop centre for all parents, providing universal access to high quality provision for children of all ages, allowing for better co-ordination of all local services for children and engaging families and communities in their organisation and development. Children's centres could build on existing best practice – the range of services already being offered in some areas by Sure Start and Early Excellence Centres. The centres would co-locate different services and offer a single place in the community where all help for parents and children could be sign-posted. Parents could have contact with a local centre for different reasons: for prospective parents to attend antenatal classes and later to attend parenting support groups; for parents to seek health advice and attend a child health clinic; for parents to find information about local services and advice about benefits; and to provide access to good quality childcare for the children of both working and non-working parents.

To date children's centres have been seen as primarily offering a future model for childcare provision. However, the model could be extended to other forms of support for parents and children. The dearth of parenting support in the UK – and the continued focus on 'failed' or 'disadvantaged' parents – could be reversed through investment in children's centres where a wide range of locally-determined support groups for parents could be seen as an integral part of children's centres.

Tackling poverty and disadvantage

Financial support for families with children, particularly those with young children, has substantially improved in recent years. Yet the persistence of high levels of poverty among families with young children (as well as projections for the impact of changes yet to be implemented) suggests that further improvements are necessary.

Given the importance of pre-pregnancy health and diet, and the difficulty of targeting a prospective parent population, the adequacy of social security support for the under 25s should be reviewed. Preconception health status is crucial in determining the wellbeing of a child. Under 25 benefit rates for single childless people should be increased to the 25-plus level.

Evidence that financial support during pregnancy can lead to better child outcomes provides a compelling argument for the introduction of financial support in recognition of pregnancy. There are two issues that need to be resolved: the method and timing of such a payment. The advantage of extending the payment of child benefit earlier into pregnancy would be its universal nature and consequently its high take-up rate (Kendall 2001; McCormick 2001). On the other hand it is difficult to imagine benefit being paid for a person whom the law does not recognise as existing in their own right (Bennett 2002). The same argument applies to the child tax credit.

An alternative approach would be an additional premium paid to pregnant women receiving income support. While some would argue that once pregnancy is confirmed the most important period for augmenting nutritional status has passed, others argue that later trimesters are also important, and that supplements given at these stages can also be effective. Qualitative research suggests parents would support a pregnancy premium that was paid from the 20th or 30th week of pregnancy (Edwards 2002).

The Sure Start Maternity Grant has now been raised to £500, closer to the actual costs associated with buying essential items for a new baby (estimated to be £565 in 1998 (Maternity Alliance, quoted in Bennett 2002)). But there is anecdotal evidence that there is confusion about whether or not parents are eligible to apply for the Sure Start Maternity Grant, particularly if they do not live in Sure Start areas (Edwards 2002). For this reason the name of the benefit should be changed.

Additional financial support should be given to large families. The UK is unusual in providing relatively more generous support for one-child families. Yet the child poverty rate among six-child household is 71 per cent, despite the fact that the largest recent fall in poverty have been among these families (Piachaud and Sutherland 2002). By 2004 over half of children in low income families will be living in large families. Greater support for large families could be achieved by increasing the payments per child (for example in the child tax credit and/or child benefit for second or subsequent children) as a priority over increasing the rates per family. For example, there is evidence to suggest that doubling the baby tax credit (paid per family and to be integrated into the child tax credit in 2003/4) would not on its own make a substantial contribution to reducing child poverty (Sutherland 2002).

In-kind support for parents could also be improved. The proposals to extend the Welfare Foods Scheme to a wider range of foods is welcome and in line with parents' own views (McCormick 2001; Edwards 2002). The change also rightly proposes equalisation of benefits between breastfeeding and non-breastfeeding mothers, although without increasing the financial value of the support there is scepticism as to whether the scheme will make a significant difference to the nutrition of poor mothers and children. However, as they stand the proposals have been described as 'a nutritional sticking plaster for the gaping wound of poverty-related health inequalities' (Maternity Alliance 2002b).

Getting the practicalities of the scheme right will be crucial to successful implementation; vouchers will need to be flexible enough to be used in different shops, including local stores and markets. The link between health advice and registration for the scheme is more contentious. While the desired outcome (better health of children and parents) is laudable, using the benefits system to try and achieve this aim is problematic. There are two concerns. Firstly, debates about poverty and relative disadvantage increasingly emphasise the importance of a (lack of) power and sense of control as a key factor in that experience. While the benefits/tax credits system is a tempting tool in the hands of governments, attempts to shape the behaviour of people reliant on it runs the risk of exacerbating the sense of powerlessness experienced by parents living in poverty, rather than increasing their sense of control.

Secondly, placing responsibility for compliance in the hands of health professionals may have an impact on the professional-client relationship. There is an understandable reluctance among health professionals to be seen to 'police' parents; indeed, for them to be seen to do so may undermine the open, trusting supportive nature of their relationship with parents. Some health visitors report anecdotally that they are willing to sign Sure Start Maternity Grant forms even when parents have not received health advice. The response to the Government's consultation on Healthy Start suggests strong philosophical (as well as practical) objections to requiring health professionals to take on this role (Maternity Alliance 2002b). Government needs to tread wearily before extending conditionality in this way.

Improving maternity and parental leave

After only six weeks of earnings-related statutory maternity pay (at 90 per cent of previous earnings) UK mothers only get flat-rate pay for 20 weeks, followed by 26 weeks unpaid leave, unless their employer offers more generous provision. In 1996 only one in five mothers received extra-statutory maternity pay (DTI 2000). Many other European countries provide payment for the whole of maternity leave and most (although not all) replace wages in full (Bradshaw and Finch 2002).

Further improvements to maternity pay are needed if the risk of poverty associated with having a child is to be reduced and mothers are to have genuine choices about whether to return to work or not in the first year of their child's life. The Government has argued that increasing the earnings-related element of pay would benefit better-paid women, who tend to return to employment anyway (DTI 2000). If this concern is widely shared replacement rates can always be paid up to a ceiling; although attempts to level inequalities via the design of maternity provision have been argued to be mistaken (Bennett 2002).

The UK is unusual in Europe in having a comparatively long period of maternity leave (much of it unpaid) and unpaid parental leave, rather than having a shorter period of better-paid maternity leave followed by paid parental leave. Bradshaw and Finch (2002) have noted that most recent developments in maternity/parenthood provision in industrialised countries have focused on parental leave more than maternity leave. The emerging evidence of the impact of fathers' earliest interactions with their children on later outcomes, outlined in this report, support this trend. While the UK's comparatively generous maternity leave entitlement is welcome, comparatively low levels of maternity pay, covering only half the leave period, mean that lower-paid women are much more likely to leave the labour market after childbirth. Because maternity leave cannot be shared with the father, a gendered division of labour is entrenched.

The UK Government must take action to encourage a more equal sharing of parental responsibilities in the first year of life. Various steps are needed. Paternity leave should be lengthened; but the priority must be to pay it at a higher level. Payment for parental leave and leave for family reasons must also be introduced; since unpaid leave is much less likely to be taken, particularly by fathers (OECD 2001).

Earnings-related payment (up to a ceiling) for parental leave should be introduced. The limit on the number of weeks of parental leave (up to a maximum level) that can be taken in the first year should be abolished. For two-parent families, once parental leave is paid, some period should be reserved for fathers. This 'daddy quota' could be given on a 'use it or lose it' basis, so that it is forgone if fathers do not take it. In Norway where an additional four weeks of parental leave is available only to fathers, use of this special quota rose to 85% in 2000 (EOC 2003). Some might argue that a 'daddy quota' already exists in the UK since parental leave is available per parent, rather than per child, but since the leave is unpaid, this provision is fairly academic.

Ultimately the ambition must be to achieve a better balance of paid leave and childcare support to enable both parents to spend time with their baby, especially during the first year of life.

Equal at One: support during pregnancy and the first 12 months

Parents (and prospective parents) should expect:

- Antenatal support that includes information about child development and preparation for the social and emotional impact of becoming a parent.
- Social, emotional and practical support in the postnatal period from a health visitor, supplemented by 'Home Visitor'-type support.
- Access to a children's centre – a place in the local community which offers a range of support during pregnancy and pre-school.
- Opportunity to influence the development of local services. Services should be driven by parents' and children's needs.
- Social security support to reduce the risk of poverty during this period.
- The opportunity for mothers and fathers to take paid leave to care for a child during the first year of life

---

The critical importance of the early months of life for a child's development requires careful consideration of the effectiveness of the public policy support provided during this period. While the UK has substantially improved its parental and early years support in recent years, there is no room for complacency. Children's life chances remain extraordinarily unequal from birth, perhaps the most significant hindrance to achieving a more socially just society. Across a wide range of existing support and services there is evidence of unmet needs.

Traditionally public policy has sought to protect the health of children and to reduce the impact of poverty. This must continue. However, growing evidence of the impact of the social and emotional context in which infants are raised – and in particular the parent-infant relationship – on child development requires us to consider the role that public policy could make in supporting parents. Enhancing support for parents during this period, through the development of group support, but also by increasing the parent-support role of existing professionals and through the development of home visitor services, would contribute to ensuring that young children have a more equal start.

Key recommendations

Reforms to midwifery and health visiting services
- Retain the number of antenatal appointments but devote a greater proportion of time to preparation for parenthood

- Increase the emphasis on social and antenatal support in health visiting and midwifery, with implications for training and recruitment

- Consider allowing direct entry into training for health visiting

- Consider redistributing health care resources and the health visitor and midwifery workforce according to measures of social deprivation.

Home Visitors
- Increasing funding to enable the kinds of volunteer and peer-to-peer schemes available in some areas to become universally available to parents in the first year of their child's life

Children's Centres
- Implement a model that combines childcare for working and non-working parents, sessional early education places, out of school care and family, parenting and health services would offer support to all parents in their local community.

Social security
- Review benefit rates for under-25s.

- Introduce a pregnancy premium.

- Raise the level of support for large families.

- Implement proposed changes to the welfare foods scheme but without extending conditionality

Leave arrangements
- Increase levels of maternity and paternity pay.

- Introduce payment for parental leave, preferably earnings-related.

- Introduce a 'daddy quota' as part of parental leave and lift restrictions on number of weeks that can be taken in the first year after the birth of a child

6. Conclusion

The evidence set out in this report demonstrates that all those who wish to achieve a more socially just society must concern themselves with reducing the unequal life chances that emerge soon after birth.

This raises difficult issues for progressive politics, such as the power of inherited privilege and the tension between parents' liberty to do the best for their children and the desire to achieve a fairer share of opportunities. Whilst these issues are beyond the scope of this book, they will need to be addressed head on if a rhetorical commitment to achieving an equal start in life for all children is to be delivered in reality.

Policy makers also face a more immediate challenge; that of the relative attention that has been given to factors that profoundly shape a child's development during and after birth. The need to prevent poverty, neglect, child abuse and deprivation is well understood. Along with protecting the health of mother and child, these have long been important public policy issues.

Less acknowledged, in public policy terms at least, is the profound impact that the parent-child relationship has on an infant's development. This is an area in which the State has chosen to tread carefully, reluctant to interfere in the private realm of family life other than in the most desperate of circumstances.

Yet if we are serious about giving children an equal start in life we can not overlook the significance of the parenting role. Public policy must be prepared to cross the threshold into the private world of the family; to consider ways in which social and emotional support for parents can be improved.

Increasing support for parents and children in this period will have a profound and long-term impact on the wellbeing of society. While an individual's development is by no means set for life, their capacity to benefit from life opportunities is significantly enhanced by positive experiences in the early months of life. Without a step change in the quantity and quality of support for parents and children during this crucial period of development, an equal start for children will remain no more than a worthy statement of ambition.

Endnotes

1   These studies were not controlled trials and excluded programmes in the US.

2   Virtually all programmes offer new or extended antenatal care including home visiting by midwives.

3   Health visitors also work with other groups of the population, particularly the elderly.

4   This was because their employment record or earnings were insufficient to qualify, because they left employment after one birth and had another baby without returning to employment, or because they did not have a job at all.

References

Acheson D (1998) *Independent Inquiry into Inequalities in Health* The Stationery Office: London

Angelsen NK, Vik T, Jacobsen G and Bakketeig LS (2001) 'Breast feeding and cognitive development at age one and five years' *Archive of Disease in Childhood* 85: 183-188

Aronen E and Kurkela S (1996) 'Long-term effects of an early home-based intervention' *Journal of the American Academy of Child and Adolescent Psychiatry* 35: 1665-1672

Audit Commission (1999) *First Assessment: A review of district nursing in England and Wales*

Avon Premature Infant Project (1998) 'Randomised trial of parental support for families with very preterm children' *Archives of Disease in Childhood Foetal Neonatal Edition* 79: 4-11

Balarajan R and Raleigh VS (1993) *Ethnicity and health. A guide for the NHS* London: Department of Health

Barker W (2002) *A developmental odyssey: children, parents and health visitors* Early Childhood Development Unit, Bristol. Presentation hosted by Tayside Primary Care NHS Trust, Dundee

Barlow J (1999) *Systematic Review of the Effectiveness of Parent Training Programmes in Improving Behavioural Problems in Children aged 3-10 years* Department of Public Health, Oxford University: Oxford

Barlow J and Coren E (2000) 'Parenting programmes for improving maternal psychosocial health (Cochrane review)' *The Cochrane Library* 4

Baydar N and Brooks-Gunn J (1991), 'Effects of Maternal Employment and Child Care Arrangements in Infancy on Preschoolers' Cognitive and Behavioral Outcomes: Evidence from the Children of the NLSY' *Developmental Psychology* 27: 918-931

Bennett F (2002) *Giving all children a good start: financial provision in pregnancy and the first year of life* Paper to IPPR First 12 Months project www.ippr.org

Bidmead C (2002) *Concept Analysis of Partnership with clients in health visiting* Unpublished paper

Blair P, Fleming P, Bensley D *et al* (1996) 'Smoking and the sudden infant death syndrome: results from 1993-5 case-control study for Confidential Enquiry into Stillbirths and Deaths in Infancy' *British Medical Journal* 313 195-198

Blanden, Gregg P and Machin S (2001) *Family Income and children's educational attainment: evidence from the NCDS and BCS* Paper presented at the IPPR child poverty conference

Boocock S (1995) 'Early childhood programs in other nations: goals and outcomes' *The Future of Children* 5.3 94-115 cited in McLoughlin J and Nagoroka J (2000) *Sooner not later: an international literature and program review of early childhood initiatives for disadvantaged families* Brotherhood of St Laurence and Centre for Community Child Health: Australia

Booth IW and Aukett MA (1997) 'Iron deficiency anaemia in infancy and early childhood' *Archives of Disease in Childhood* 76: 549-554

Bradshaw J (2001a) (ed) *Poverty: the outcomes for children* Family Policy Studies Centre: London

Bradshaw J (2001b) 'Child poverty under Labour' in Fimister G (ed) *An End in Sight? Tackling child poverty in the UK* Child Poverty Action Group: London

Bradshaw and Finch N (2002) *A Comparison of Child Benefit Packages in 22 Countries* Department for Work and Pensions Research Report 174, Corporate Document Services: Leeds

Buchan L, Clemerson J and Davis H (1998) 'Working with families of children with special needs: the parent adviser scheme' *Child Care, Health and Development* 14: 81-91

Burghes l, Clarke L and Cronin N (1997) *Fathers and fatherhood in Britain* Family Policy Studies Centre: London

Carroli G, Villar J, Piaggio G, Khan-Neelofur D, Gulmezoglu M, Mugford M, Lumbiganon P, Farnot U and Bersgio P (2001) 'WHO systematic review of randomized controlled trials of routine antenatal care' *The Lancet* 357 1565-1570

Caughy MO, DiPietro J, Strobino D (1994) 'Day-Care Participation as a Protective Factor in the Cognitive Development of Low Income Children' *Child Development* 65: 457-471

Chase Lansdale PL, Gordon RA, Brooks-Gunn J and Klebanor PK 'Neighbourhood and Family Influences on the Intellectual and Behavioral Competence of Pre-school and Early School Age Children' in Brooks-Gunn *et al* (eds) (1997) *Neighbourhood Poverty: Context and Consequences for Children* Russell Sage Foundation: New York

Chugani HT (1997) 'Neuroimaging of developmental non-linearity and development pathologies' in Thatcher RW, Lyon GR, Rumsey J and Krasnegor N (eds) *Developmental Neuro-imaging: Mapping the*

Development of Brain and Behavior San Diego Academic Press: San Diego

Clarke P, Allen C, Law C, Shiell A, Godfrey K, Barker D (1998) 'Weight gain in pregnancy and blood pressure in childhood' *British Journal of Obstetrics and Gynaecology* 101: 398-403

Cowan CP and Cown PA (2000) *When partners become parents* Presentation to PC2000: an international symposium London

Cragg A, Dickens S, Taylor C, Henricson C and Keep G (2002) *Reaching parents: producing and delivering parent information resources – a qualitative research study and practice guide* National Family and Parenting Institute: London

Cummings EM, Davies PT, Campbell SB (2000) *Developmental Psychopatholgy and Family Process: theory, research and clinical implications* Guildford Press: New York

Curtice L (1989) *The First Year of Life: Promoting the health of babies in the community* Maternity Alliance

Czeizel AE (1999) 'Ten years of experience in periconceptional care' *European Journal of Obstetrics, Gynaecology and Reproductive Biology* 84, 43-49

Davis H and Ali Choudry P (1987) 'Helping Bangladeshi families: the Parent Advisor Scheme' *Mental Handicap* 16: 48-51

Dawson G, Ashman SB, Carver LJ 'The role of early experience in shaping behavioural and brain developments and its implications for social policy' *Developmental Psychopathology* 12.4: 695-712

Daycare Trust (2003) 'Parents need more help from Government' Press release, 30 January www.daycaretrust.org.uk

Delvaux T and Buekens P (1999) 'Disparity in prenatal care in Europe: study group on barriers and incentives to prenatal care in Europe' *European Journal of Obstetrics and Gynaecology and Reproductive Biology* 83.2: 185-190

Department of Health (1997) *Survey of infant feeding in Asian families: early feeding practices and growth* The Stationery Office

Department of Health (2001) *Children and Young People on Child Protection Registers: year ending 31 March 2001*

Department of Health (2001) *NHS Hospital and Community Health Services non-medical workforce census*

Department of Health (2002) *NHS Hospital and Community Health services non-medical staff in England 1991-2001*

Department of Health (2002) *Vacancies Survey March 2002*

Department of Health (2002) *Healthy Start: proposals for reform of the Welfare Food Scheme*

Doyle W and Rees G (2001) 'Maternal malnutrition in the UK and low birth weight' *Nutrition and Health* 15: 213-218

Drever F and Whitehead M (ed) (1997) *Health Inequalities: Series DS 15* Government Statistical Service, The Stationery Office: London

DTI (2000) *Work and Parents: Competitiveness and Choice: Research and Analysis* Department of Trade and Industry.

Duncan G and Chase-Landsdale (2000) *Welfare Reform and Child Wellbeing* Northwestern University

Edwards L (2002) *The First Twelve Months: The parent perspective* Focus group research with parents of babies under 12 months www.ippr.org

Elbourne D, Oakley A and Chalmers I (1989) 'Social and psychological support during pregnancy' in The Cochrane Database of Systematic Reviews, *The Cochrane Library 2* 1998 Update Software (updated quarterly): Oxford

Elkan R, Blair M and Robinson J (2000) 'Evidence-based practice and health visiting; the need for theoretical underpinnings for evaluation' *Journal of Advanced Nursing* 31.6: 1316-1323

EOC (2003) *Dads on dads: needs and expectations at home and at work* Equal Opportunities Commission.

Ermisch J, Francesconi F and Pevalin D (2001) *Outcomes for children of poverty* Institute for Social and Economic Research, Department for Work and Pensions Research Report 158

Esping Anderson G (2003) 'Unequal opportunities and social inheritance' in Corak M (ed) forthcoming *The Dynamics of Intergenerational Income Mobility* Cambridge University Press

Evans R (2002) *Interpreting and Addressing Inequalities in Health: From Black to Acheson to Blair to...?* Office of Health Economics: London

Feinstein L (1998) *Pre-school Education Inequality?* Centre for Economic Performance, London School of Economics: London

Foster M (1988) 'The French Puericultrice' *Children and Society* 4: 319-334

Frost N, Johnson L, Stein M and Wallis L (2000) 'Home-Start and the delivery of family support' *Children and Society* 14: 328-342

Ghate D and Hazel N (2002) *Parenting in Poor Environments: Stress, support and coping* Jessica Kingsley: London

Gibbons J and Thorpe S (1998) 'Can voluntary support projects help vulnerable families? The work of Home-Start' *British Journal of Social Work* 19: 189-202

Gillies V and Edwards R (2003) *Support for parenting: the views of parents of 8-12 year old children* Resources in parenting: access to capitals project. Families and Social Capital ESRC Research Group, South Bank University.

Gissler M and Hemminki E (1994) 'Amount of antenatal care and infant outcome' *European Journal of Obstetrics and Gynaecology and Reproductive Biology* 56: 9-14

Gomby D (1999) 'Understanding evaluations of home visitation programs' *The Future of Children* 9.1: 27-43

Gomby D, Culross P and Behrman R (1999) 'Home visiting: recent program evaluation – analysis and recommendations' in *The Future of Children* 9.1 cited in McLoughlin and Nagorka J (2000) *Sooner not later: an international literature and program review of early childhood initiatives for disadvantaged families* Brotherhood of St Laurence and Centre for Community Child Health: Australia

Gregg P, Harkness S and Machin S (1999) *Child Development and Family Income* Joseph Rowntree Foundation

Haas L (1992) *Equal parenthood and social policy – a study of parental leave in Sweden* State University of New York: Albany NY

Hall D (2001) *Health For All Children* Paper to Royal College of Surgeons

Harris P (2002) 'Welfare rewritten' in *Journal of Social Policy* 31.3: 314

Hart B and Risley TR (1995) *Meaningful Differences in the Everyday Experience of Young American Children* Paul H Brookes Publishing: Baltimore

Health Statistics Quarterly 12 (2001) The Stationery Office: London

Hemminiki E, Blondel B and Study Group on Barriers and Incentives to Prenatal Care in Europe (2001) 'Antenatal care in Europe: varying ways of providing high-coverage services' *European Journal of Obstetrics and Gynaecology and Reproductive Biology* 94.1: 145-148

Henricson C, Katz I, Mesie J, Sandison M and Tunstill J (2001) *National Mapping of Family Services in England and Wales – a consultation document* National Family and Parenting Institute.

Hill MS and Jenkins SP (1999) 'Poverty among British children: chronic or transitory?' in Bradbury B, Mickelwright J and Jenkins J *Falling in, Climbing Out: the dynamics of child poverty in industrialised countries* UNICEF

HM Treasury (1999) *The Modernisation of Britain's Tax and Benefit System 4: Tackling poverty and extending opportunity*

HM Treasury/DTI (2003) *Balancing work and family life: enhancing choice and support for parents*

Hobcraft J (2002) 'Social exclusion and the generations' in Hills J, Le Grand J and Piachaud D (eds) *Understanding social exclusion* Oxford University Press

Hoddinott P and Pill R (1999) 'Qualitative study of decisions about infant feeding among women in the east end of London' *British Medical Journal* 318: 30-34

Hodnett E (1998) 'Support from caregivers during at-risk pregnancy' in The Cochrane Database of Systematic Reviews *The Cochrane Library* 2 Update Software (updated quarterly): Oxford

Hodnett E and Roberts I (1998) 'Home-based social support for socially disadvantaged mothers' in The Cochrane Database of Systematic Reviews *The Cochrane Library 2* Update Software (updated quarterly): Oxford

Hoffman LW, Youngblade LM, Coley AS, Fuligni AS and Dovacs DD (1999) *Mothers at work: effects on children's wellbeing* Cambridge Studies in Social and Emotional Development, Cambridge University Press: Cambridge

Holden J, Sagovsky R and Cox J (1989) 'Counselling in a general practice setting: a controlled study of health visitor intervention in the treatment of postnatal depression' *British Medical Journal* 298: 223-226

Home Office (1998) *Supporting Families* The Stationery Office

Home Office (2003) *Reducing Homicide: a review of possibilities* On-line report by Fiona Brockman and Mike Maguire, January www.homeoffice.gov.uk

Home Office (2001) *Criminal Statistics: England and Wales 1999* The Stationery Office: London

Home Start UK (2000) *Survey of new parents* www.home-start.org.uk

James 0 (2002) *They ***k you up* Bloomsbury: London

Jefferis B, Power C and Hertzman C (2002) 'Birth weight, childhood socioeconomic environment and cognitive development in the 1958 British birth cohort study' *British Medical Journal* 325: 305-8

Joshi H and Verropoulou G (2000) *Maternal Employment and Child Outcomes: Analysis of two Birth Cohort Studies* The Smith Institute, London

Kehrer B and Wolin V (1979) 'Impact of income maintenance on low birthweight: evidence from the Gary experiment' *Journal of Human Resources* 14: 434-462

Kendall L (2001) 'Pregnant mothers should get child benefit' *New Statesman* 12 February

Kendall L and Harker L (2002) *From Welfare to Wellbeing: the future of social care* IPPR: London.

Kiernan K (1996) 'Lone Motherhood, Employment and Outcomes for Children' *Journal of Law, Policy and the Family* 10: 233-256

Kitzman H, Olds D, Henderson C, Hanks C, Cole R, Tatelbaum R, McConnochie K, Sidora K, Luckey D, Shaver D, Engelbardt K, James D and Barnard K (1997) 'Effect of prenatal and infancy home visitation by nurses on pregnancy outcomes, childhood injuries and repeated childbearing: a randomized controlled trial' *Journal of the American Medical Association* 278: 644-652

Kraemer S (1995) 'What are fathers for?' in Burck C and Speed B (eds) (1995) *Gender, power and relationships* Routledge: London

Kuh D and Ben-Shlomo Y (eds) (1997) *A life course approach to chronic disease epidemiology* Oxford University Press: Oxford

La Valle I, Arthur S, Millward C, Scott J and Clayden M (2002) *Happy Families? Atypical work and its influence on family life* Policy Press: Oxford

Lamb ME (ed) (1986) *The Father's Role: Applied Perspectives* J Wiley: New York

Lamb ME (1996) *What are fathers for?* Presentation at Men and their Children conference, IPPR

Lenton S (2000) *Improving the health of mothers and babies* A summary of the evidence to support antenatal and perinatal screening, with recommendations for change.

Lindmark G and Cnattingius S (1991) *The scientific basis of antenatal care* Report from a state-of-the-art conference. Acta Obstet. Gynaecol. Scand. 70: 105-109. [does this mean something??]

Logue ME (2001) *Implications of Brain Development Research for Even Start Family Literacy Programs* US Department for Education

Lord Chancellor's Department (2002) *Moving Forward Together: A proposed strategy for marriage and relationship support for 2002 and beyond* Advisory Group on Marriage and Relationship Support

MacArthur C *et al* (2002) 'Effects of redesigned community postnatal care on women's health four months after birth: a cluster randomized controlled trial' *The Lancet* 359 2 February

Margetts BM, Mohd Yusof S, Al Dallal Z and Jackson AA (2002) 'Persistence of lower birth weight in second generation South Asian babies born in the United Kingdom' *Journal of Epidemiology and Community Health* 56: 684-687

Maternity Alliance (2002a) 'Preconception care' *Maternity Action* 90

Maternity Alliance (2002b) Notes of Healthy Start consultation meeting, 21 November

McAllister F (ed) (1995) *Marital breakdown and the health of the nation* One Plus One: London

McCormick J (2001) *Early Endowment: Investing better in pregnancy and infancy* Scottish Council Foundation.

McCulloch A and Joshi HE (1999) 'Child Development and Family Resources: an exploration of evidence from the second generation of the 1958 British Birth Cohort' Institute for Social and Economic Research Working Paper, University of Essex

McDuffie R, Beck A, Bischoff K, Corss, J and Orleans M (1996) 'Effect of prenatal care visits on perinatal outcome among low risk women' *JAMA* 275: 847-851

Mental Health Foundation (2002) *From pregnancy to early childhood: early interventions to enhance the mental health of children and families* April 2002

Middleton S, Ashworth K and Braithwaite I (1997) *Small Fortunes: spending on children, childhood poverty and parental sacrifice* Joseph Rowntree Foundation

Moore K *et al* (1999) *A Birth Cohort Study, Conceptual and Design Considerations and Rationale* Prepared for the US Department of Education, Office of Educational Research and Improvement, and the National Center for Education Statistics

Moorman A and Ball M (2001) *Understanding parents needs* National Family and Parenting Institute: London

MORI (1999) Parents survey conducted on behalf of the National Family and Parenting Institute: London

Moss P and Deven F (eds) (1999) *Parental Leave: Progress or Pitfall* CBGS: Brussels

Mount F (1982) *The subversive family: an alternative history of love and marriage* Cape: London

Naish J (2002) *Health Inequalities and children under one: the contribution of health services* Paper presented to IPPR seminar on health inequalities and children under one, 27 June www.ippr.org

NCT (2000) *Access to maternity information and support: the experiences and needs of women before and after giving birth* National Childbirth Trust

NICHD Early Child Care Research Network (1997) 'The Effects of Infant Child Care on Infant -Mother Attachment Security: Results of the NICHD Study of Early Child Care' *Child Development* 68: 860-879

Nobes G and Smith M (1997) 'Physical Punishment of Children in Two Parent Families' *Clinical Child Psychology and Psychiatry* 2.2:271-281

NSPCC (2002) *Submission to the Department of Health on the National Service Framework for Children* July 2002

Nursing and Midwifery Council (2002) *Statistical Analysis of the Register 1 April 2001 to 31 March 2002* November

Oakley A (1992) *Social support and motherhood* Blackwell: Oxford

Oakley A, Hickey O, Rajan L, Hickey A (1996) 'Social support in pregnancy: does it have long term effects?' *Journal of Reproductive Infant Psychology* 14: 7-22

OECD (2001) Employment Outlook 2001, Organisation for Economic Co-operation and Development.

ONS (1997) *Health Inequalities* Decennial Supplement 15: London

ONS (1997) *Mortality Statistics: childhood, infant and perinatal 30* London

ONS (2000) *Births, perinatal and infant mortality statistics 2000* London

Olds D, Eckenrode J, Henderson C *et al* (1997) 'Long-term effects of home visitation on maternal life course and child abuse and neglect. Fifteen-year follow-up of a randomised trial' *Journal of the American Medical Association* 278: 637-643

Page A (2002) *Changing times: support for parents and families during pregnancy and the first twelve months* Paper to IPPR seminar, 9 July www.ippr.org

Parke (1996) *Fatherhood* from the Developing Child Series Harvard University Press: Cambridge, Mass

Patterson J, Barlow J, Mockford C, Klimes I, Pyper C and Stewart-Brown S (2002) 'Improving mental health through parenting programmes:

block randomized controlled trial' *Archives of Disease in Childhood* 87: 472-77

Patterson J, Barlow J, Stewart-Brown S, Mockford C, Klimes I and Pyper C (2001) *Improving mental health among children and their parents through parenting programmes in general practice: A randomized controlled trial* HSRU: Oxford

Patterson J, Mockford C, Barlow J, Pyper C and Stewart-Brown S (2002) 'Need and demand for parenting programmes in general practice' *Archives of Disease in Childhood* 87: 486-71

Piachaud D and Sutherland H (2002) *Changing poverty post-1997* CASE paper 63 Centre for Analysis of Social Exclusion

Plewis I, Smith G, Wright G and Cullis A (2001) *Linking child poverty and child outcomes: exploring data and research strategies* Working Paper 1, Department for Work and Pensions

Pugh G and De'Ath E (1984) *The Needs of Parents: policy and practice in parent education* National Children Bureau: London

Pugh G, De'Ath E and Smith C (1994) *Confident Parents, Confident Children: Policy and practice in parent education and support* National Children Bureau: London

Rajan L, Turner H and Oakley A (1996) *A study of Home Start* Social Sciences Research Unit, University of London

Ravelli A, van der Meulen J, Michels R *et al* (1998) 'Glucose tolerance in adults after prenatal exposure to the Dutch famine' *The Lancet* 351: 173-177

Reading R (1997) 'Social disadvantage and infection in children' *Sociology of Health and Illness* 19.4: 395-414

Richards M, Hardy R, Kuh D, Wadsworth MEJ (2001) 'Birth weight and cognitive function in the British 1946 birth cohort: longitudinal population study' *British Medical Journal* 322: 199-203 (27 January)

Roberts H (1997) 'Socio-economic determinants of health: children, inequalities and health' *British Medical Journal* 314: 1122

Rosenzwig MR and Wolpin KI (1994) 'Are there increasing returns to intergenerational production of human capital? Maternal schooling and child intellectual development' *Journal of Human Resources* 29: 670-693.

Ross DP and Roberts P (1999) *Income and Child Wellbeing: a new perspective on the poverty debate* Canadian Council on Social Development

Royal College of Obstetricians and Gynaecologists (1982) *Report of the RCOG working party on antenatal intrapartum care: Appendix 2*

Salmon D, Hook G and Haywood M (2002) *An evaluation of the post of Specialist Health Visitor in Infant Mental Health* Bristol North Primary Care Trust and Faculty of Health and Social Care, University of the West of England.

Sanders MR, Montgomery DT and Brechman-Toussaint ML (2000) 'The mass media and the prevention of child behaviour problems: the evaluation of a television series to promote positive outcomes for parents and their children' *Journal of Child Psychology and Psychiatry* 41.7: 939-948

Saxena S, Majeed A and Jones M (1999) 'Socio-economic differences in childhood consultation rates in general practice in England and Wales: prospective cohort study' *British Medical Journal* 318 (7184): 642-658.

Schweinhart L, Barnes H, Weikart D *et al* (1993) 'Significant benefits: the High/Scope Perry Pre-school Study through age 27' *Monographs of the High/Scope Educational Research Foundation* 10

Scott S, Spender Q, Doolan M, Jacobs B and Aspland H (2001) 'Multicentre controlled trial of parenting groups for childhood antisocial behaviour in clinical practice' *British Medical Journal* 323: 1-7.

Seeley S, Murray L and Cooper P (1996) 'The outcome for mothers and babies of health visitor intervention' *Health Visitor* 69: 135-138

Shonkoff JP and Phillips DA (eds) (2000) *Neurons to Neighbourhoods* Committee on Integrating the Science of Early Childhood Development, Board on Children, Youth and Families, National Research Council and Institute of Medicine, National Academy Press, Washington DC

Singh D and Newburn M (2000) *Women's Experiences of Postnatal Care* National Childbirth Trust

Singhal A, Cole TJ and Lucas A (2001) 'Early nutrition in preterm infants and later blood pressure: two cohorts after randomised trials' *The Lancet* 357: 413-19

Smith M (1995) *A Community Study of Physical Violence to Children in the Home and Associated Variables* Poster presented at ISPCAN 5th European Conference on Child Abuse and Neglect: Oslo

Spencer N (2000) (2nd edition) *Poverty and Child Health* Radcliffe: Oxford

Spooner A (2001) 'Can GPs still identify children at risk? What is our role?' *British Journal of General Practice* 329

Sutherland H (2002) *One parent families, poverty and labour policy* National Council for One Parent Families

Thatcher RW, Lyon GR, Rumsey J and Krasnegor N (eds) (1997) *Developmental Neuro-imaging: Mapping the Development of Brain and Behavior* San Diego Academic Press: San Diego

Thomas P, Golding J and Peters T (1991) 'Delayed antenatal care: does it effect pregnancy outcome?' *Social Science and Medicine* 32: 715-723

Underdown D (2000) *When Feeding Fails* London

Webster-Stratton C, Hollinsworth T and Kolpacoff M (1989) 'The long-term effectiveness and clinical significance of three cost-effective training programs for families with conduct problem children' *Journal of Consulting and Clinical Psychology* 57.4: 550-553

Webster-Stratton C and Hammon M (1997) 'Treating children with early-onset conduct problems: a comparison of child and parent training interventions' *Journal of Consulting and Clinical Psychology* 65.1: 93-109

Werner E (1997) 'Vulnerable but invincible: high-risk children from birth to adulthood' *Paediatric Supplement* 422: 103-105 cited in McLoughlin J and Nagorka J (2000) *Sooner not later: an international literature and program review of early childhood initiatives for disadvantaged families* Brotherhood of St Laurence and Centre for Community Child Health: Australia

Wilson H (2002) 'Brain Science, early intervention and 'at risk' families: implications for parents, professionals and social policy' *Social Policy and Society* 1.3: 191-202

Wolfendale S and Einzig H (eds.) (1999) *Parenting education and support: new opportunities* David Fulton: London